Listening Inside the Dance:
A Life in Maine Infused with Tango

*P*oems
Elizabeth W. Garber

With selections translated into Spanish
By
Demian Gawianski

The Illuminated Sea Press
2005

Copyright © 2005 by Elizabeth W. Garber

Design, Cover and Illustrations by Catlin Sayers Barnes
www.fenicedesign.com

Front Cover Painting of "Illuminated Sea" © Brita Holmquist
Front Cover Painting of "Tango Postcard" © James Strickland

"For Some Reason" published in Off the Coast, September 2005

All Poems and translations of Jorge Luis Borges
from *Selected Poems*,
Ed. By Alexander Coleman, Penguin Books 1999
From the Prologue of *Los Conjurados* translated by Willis Barnstone.
From the poem "Break of Day" translated by Stephen Kessler.
From the poem "Dream" translated by Alexander Coleman.

Printed in Maine by Alliance Press, Brunswick, Maine

ISBN 0- 9761311-2-9

The Illuminated Sea Press
66 Miller St.
Belfast, Maine 04915
illuminatedseapress.com

Dedicated to the treasures of my heart
My children Gabriel and Miriam

∼

And to my friend Martha Derbyshire
In gratitude for your deep listening into our lives

Contents:

Listening Inside the Body — 1

Riding This Horse	2
Late Summer in an Election Year	3
Going Away to a Rented Summer House the First Cold Night of Fall	4
Americans Become Refugees One at a Time	6
Continuing to Explore How to Position Myself in Regards to the to the Leaf of Happiness	7
Applied Poetry	8
The List	10
Occupying the Mind	12
Living in the Museum of Snowstorms: Winter Haiku	13
Remembering the Fatherlands	14
There's Nothing Like a Flu	15
The New Marriage	16
A New Kind of Proposal	17
The Grant Proposal	18
That Question We Each Carry	19
The Best Ex-Husband You Could Ever Ask For	20
It is Important to Forget	22
The Morning My Inner Dog Woke Me Up	23
Winter Takes Its Toll	24
The Smell of Wildness	25
The Seduction	26
Bertha: A Story That Followed Me Home	28
For Some Reason	30
Crush	31

Listening Inside the Dance   32
Poems translated into Spanish by Demian Gawianski

The Night Plane to Buenos Aires	34
El Avión Nocturno a Buenos Aires	35
A Man Awake	36
Un Hombre Despierto	37
Buenos Aires	38
Buenos Aires	40
Ode to Dulce de Leche	42
Oda al Dulce de Leche	44
First Lesson with Eladia at El Beso	46
Primera Clase con Eladia en El Beso	47
The Voices in Your Ear in the Beginning Class	48
Las Voces que se Oyen en la Primera Clase	49
Being a Beginner	50
Ser Principiante	51
Generosity	52
Generosidad	53
Waiting For My Teacher	54
Esperando a Mi Maestro	55
My Daughter at the Milonga	56
Mi Hija en la Milonga	58
Finding My Teacher	60
Buscando a Mi Maestro	61
The First Teacher	62
La Primera Profesora	63
The Panther	64
La Pantera	66
Making "The Cross"	68
Haciendo "El Cruce"	69

The Smell of an Evening	70
El Olor de un Atardecer	71
A City of Kisses	70
Una Ciudad de Besos	71
The Conversation We Do Not Have	72
La Conversación Que No Tenemos	73
Released From Smiling	74
Exentos de Sonreír	75
The Relief of Rain	74
El Alivio de la Lluvia	75
Sunday Afternoon Tango Lesson in the Sala of Our B&B	76
Clase de Tango en la Sala de Nuestro Hospedaje, un Sábado por la Tarde	77
Listening Inside the Dance (Even Beginners Can Discover Tango Bliss)	78
Escuchando la Danza (Aún los Principiantes Pueden Descubrir la Dicha del Tango)	79
The Last Morning Before We Leave	80
La Mañana Anterior a Nuestra Partida	81

Bringing the Dance Home 83

North Atlantic Tango Practice	84
Returning Home to Discover Exile	85
Traveling Through Cultures of Eyes	86
Un Viaje por las Culturas de los Ojos	88
Rediscovering Myself in Borges' Dream, Again and Again	90
What the Acupuncturist Discovers in Tango	92
Learning the Boleo	93
Take This Vow	94
Lilac Night	95

The Day After She Finishes Driver's Ed My Daughter Suddenly Notices I Write Poetry While Driving	96

Listening Inside Island Time — 97

Listening Inside Island Time	98
Stories From the Island at the Edge of the World	101
It's So Good We Didn't Get What We Thought We Always Wanted	103
The Different Sizes of Silence	104

The Time It Takes — 105

The Time It Takes For the Work to Become Effortless	106

About The Author — 108

About The Translator — 108

Acknowledgements — 109

Listening Inside the Body

"After all these years I have observed that beauty, like happiness, is frequent. A day does not pass when we are not, for an instant, in paradise."

— Jorge Luis Borges

Riding This Horse

For the first fifty years,
we ride this horse like there's no tomorrow.
Then one day, we round a bend
and find ourselves careening downhill,
trying to put on the skids,
an outrage of fury and grief covering the fear,
"I don't remember signing on for this!"

At first, many are enraged by the aches,
aghast at the flowering of creases at the eyes.
Will we be like some aging cabaret singer, our lipstick
snaking out along our wrinkles?

Suddenly our women friends are dressing like eccentric aunts,
and the men like dapper odd uncles with hair
fuzzy and unruly sticking out under hats with ear flaps.

I think the worst fears hit in our fifties,
like the worst fears of winter come in August.
Once you get to 20 below, you just put on your layers,
and head right out into it.

It takes a finer skill to ride a horse well
going down the mountain.

My table is set with a banquet of seventy year olds.
Jo, my mom, takes her aspirin and heads off to kick boxing class.
My aunt Wa, wrestling with emphysema,
heads out at 5 below, to split a little wood.
My cousin Kate, nestled in on her ridge,
writes into the heart of the world.
My friend Diane heads into her studio each day
to assemble the mysteries into form.
Even though she aches each time she goes to stand,
she whispers to me, radiant amidst the treasures in her studio,
"My seventies are really the best! What is most important is so clear now."

As they ride this horse like there's no tomorrow.

Late Summer in an Election Year

at the ocean, the air hangs heavy
with the scent of wild roses.
each blossom agitated and trembling,
two frantic competing bees jostling
in this small palm of pink silk.

the beach is weary with footprints,
supine, waiting for the creeping tide
to wash it smooth.

in the gardens, the earwigs have scoured
the hostas into chaotic lace.
the lamb's ears wilted and limp
wait for frost.

in town, the bumper stickers
wage a silent war.
the mail brings my son's required
registration for selective service.

coming home, all I want to do
is cut ripe peaches into indigo bowls,
add a flurry of blueberries picked yesterday,
and draw my teenagers out of the house
to sit in the quiet garden to eat
in this sad sweet light of morning.

Going Away to a Rented Summer House the First Cold Night of Fall

There is so much quiet in a borrowed house,
stepping into a stranger's collection
of art books and novels high
beside the worn soft leather couches.

Stepping into this realm of objects carefully placed,
the owners' absence so penetrating,
their choices so persistent,
it's hard to remember my own life.

I start to wonder, how old am I now?
Am I twenty, house-sitting for one of my professors?
I start to forget, what do I know how to do now?
Did I ever figure out what I was going to do in my life?

I enter this young self I always thought I was,
when I was so lost and wandering,
spending time in grown-up's houses,
wondering what my house would be like when I grew up.

I can't take off my jacket.
There is nothing I am supposed to do.
I have stepped out of my world and all that calls me so urgently,
to slip into this quiet where there is no trace of my life.

I begin to read a book of Buddhist quotations for each day of the year.
By the time I get to March,
it seems I have always been sitting in this chair,
looking out into the late October dusk,
the heavy laden gray clouding over the pine-etched islands,
the sea settling into impenetrable vastness.

The anchors of my carefully constructed life vanish.
The outlines of the granite shoreline
disappear into the rising dark,
behind this lamp's glow of warmth.

When I pause to watch this solitary light,
the darkness snug against the glass,
my old friend loneliness appears,
as if she's been lying in wait.

Before this old longing can settle in with its familiar ache,
I start wondering into this presence.
Who have I been missing all this time?
What do I mean by loneliness?

The word starts breaking into tiny fragments, scattering
like ash floating off the log as I stoke the fire.
How can I be lonely
when I am here,
sitting in this soft chair beside the dark sea
eating my bowl of steamed kale
picked from my garden this afternoon?

At the edge of my bowl,
there is a minute movement.
A tiny brilliant green inchworm
has followed me here to circumnavigate my plate.

How can I be anything
but smiling gently,
finding myself here?

Americans Become Refugees One at a Time

They say most Americans are one major illness away
from landing out in the streets, homeless,
abandoned, to live an invisible life from their cars.
Americans become refugees one at a time.

Our right to the pursuit of happiness
has allowed us to be hunted down by every corporation,
strip-mining Americans for our money, our time, our history.
Our teens are besieged for enlistment,
brainwashed out of wisdom,
fattened for the slaughter of innocence,
pursued by a hunger so enormous
they take razors to their arms to ease the pain.

You may wake up and find that Nestlé has bought your town's water,
or that Monsanto's genetically altered seed has invaded your cornfield.
They will sue you for patent violation and you will lose the case
and maybe your family's farm.
The hidden sniper waits to pick us off one at a time.

Nearly everyone I know can't afford health insurance.
Nearly everyone I know doesn't make enough to save for retirement.
We are growing older in a time of precarious balance,
when a flood of conservative millionaires believe
if you don't have money, morally, it's your fault.
They are on a mission to strip and destroy
Social Security and the health and welfare of the poor,
so we can feel the pain of deserving our poverty.

After going round the world, assassinating every last great hope,
turning countries into concentration camps for a cheaper sneaker,
they have brought the trained conspirators home to turn on us.
The coup was bloodless, masterminded with computers,
the vote snatched out of our hands, the numbers manipulated
as easily as spoiled kids stealing grades from the principal's office.

We are living at the end of an empire,
careening toward collapse, and they loot us
like clouds of crows descending on a cornfield, feeding off the top.
Do we each hope we will somehow manage to slip through unscathed?
Are we Odysseus sailing between the horrifying jaws of Skylla
and the sucking vortex of Charybdis,
sacrificing his brave companions on the journey home,
to wash up on the beach alone, weeping beside the wreckage?
Or will we grasp onto the hands of our companions
hard enough so that we are not separated in the storm,
discovering new ways to strengthen each other as we head into a time
that is beyond our knowing?

Continuing to Explore How to Position Myself in Regards to the Leaf of Happiness

wating for a leaf
standing under lush oak tree
breeze meditation

pale yellow leaves fall
down through dark pine maze of trunks
glimpsing light, floating

leaves pass right by me
I forget to reach and grab
watch it fall and smile

fear of November
disappears, smelling forest
like a happy dog

Applied Poetry

Lovers may think they are the only ones
to discover the poetry living below their fingertips,
but theirs is an unrecorded epic
of their own discovery.
Not knowing the ancient Asian mariners
charted these landscapes of the body,
mapping the contours of ankle and brow.
Naming each inlet, every curve in the river
as thoroughly as the explorers that school children
memorize, Cabot, Cartier, Champlain,
as they followed the coastline of the St. Lawrence.

For nearly 5,000 years, this poetry has been named,
but each day, each hour, we discover a new poem.
Our smooth fingertips stroke the minute hollows
before the tiny flame of steel,
wrapped with silver or copper handles,
lights up the poetry of our moment in this body.
The tangles of life come unraveled,
the blocked culverts are reopened,
the spring rivulets stream clear.
As good as the best poetry reading ever,
this applied poetry lights up the eyes,
brightens the cheeks,
deepens the breath,
brings the sigh,
releases a jewel of a tear,
and then laughter is reawakened.

Take yourself on a little journey.
You can do it right now and no one will know.
You are leaping from poem to poem with your fingertips.
No one will know that in the solid satisfying dent
on the cresting top of your skull
the wise ones converge and you can visit them
at "The One Hundred Meetings," inviting them to
clear the chaos of your mind.

You can rub your forefinger and thumb at the crease in your brow,
as if thinking deeply, enough to impress any bystander,
not knowing you are "Collecting Bamboo,"
your eyebrows becoming a forest of a calligrapher's stroked leaves.

In the hollow in front of your ears,
just open your jaw halfway and you'll step right into
"The Listening Palace." Enter bowing.
Bring the poetry of your life and no wearied news.
Bring the fresh sounds of spring peepers from the marsh,
and not the lies of advertising,
to honor this palace of your own listening.

You can travel in any direction, finding the road map
just right for your journey.
Some points are practical workhorses of honesty.
"Wrist Bone," "Joining the Valley," "Returning Current."
Others rival heaven, "Cloud Gate," "Amidst Elegance,"
and who could miss the opening of their "Abundant Splendor"?

After the hollow below my inside anklebone was awakened,
I walked to the crest of the hill in my little town,
and the bay spreading out before me at dawn
became "The Illuminated Sea,"
a joy reawakened each day.

These brief bold piercing moments of verse teach us.
Happiness is only a moment away,
just pull back the veil.
It is on the other side of right now,
it is only a moment away.
This is our original face,
the one we were born with,
the delight we can reawaken
from our long falling asleep,
in this body, this good body
filled with poetry.

The List

Most single women I know have made
many more than one. It may be one of the most active
vestiges of magic in our culture, the making
of the list that has every quality that you want in a partner.

They are hidden in the backs of journals,
next to bedside lamps, and years ago
when I was newly married, my husband
shyly pulled out his well-edited list
from under the blotter on his busy desk.

So maybe I shouldn't have been surprised
when my thirteen year old daughter referred
to hers. In a rare moment of confiding,
she said, "It's so awkward mom.
There are these boys who like me."

I asked what did she think of some of them.
"Well, none of them meet my three standards."
"What are those?" I asked with curiosity.
"They have to be funny, responsible,
and they have to be independent thinkers.
I hate passive people!"

"So, some of them are 1s, some are 2s,
but none are all three."
"So what are you going to do?" I asked.
She looked at me incredulously.
"Nothing. None of them meet my standards!"

In another moment of grace, I heard this year's version.
Nearly fifteen, in love with ballroom dancing,
she can tell a rumba from a mambo beat in the songs on the radio
and dances those steps in her sneakers in the car
as I drive her to school at 7:15 a.m.

She's now "looking for someone to move here from away,
who's a really good dancer, and who has a good frame."
Of course, I don't know what that means.
"You know, like really good tango dancers, mom,
how they stand, with their arms out, and back straight.
That's a good frame! And he has to be a Democrat or Green,
and be muy divertido!" and she grabs her backpack,
leaps out of the car, smiling good-bye.

Traveling by train in England last spring with my daughter,
I read an interview with a woman novelist
who was asked, "Who is the love of your life?"
In that split second pause when I imagined all of the readers
scanning their own lives with a quick wondering evaluation,
she answered with simple clarity, "My daughter."

Looking across at my daughter on the train,
or at my son when he's home on break from college,
or even now, watching the gulls covering the winter moorings,
all heads down looking out to sea as I walk by them on the early snow,
it becomes clear.
We are to love who is here,
as the love of our life,
rather than the one we long for,
the one we try to sculpt out of our desiring.

Occupying the Mind

On the long childhood journeys to my grandmother's farm,
crossing Ohio, the VW bus struggling up each hill,
shuddering in the wind, we ate deviled eggs
and played as many games of Go Fish and Authors
as we could stand. Then my little brothers lay down on their sides
driving little matchbox cars in the way back. I was left,
stretched out on the seat, watching the endless lines of branches
scratching across the heavy Midwestern November skies.
The emptiness of my mind was more than I could stand.
I couldn't bear that I was still only thirteen
and there was so little to think about as I faced another six hours of enduring.
My mind seemed as dull as this vast landscape of fields and woods.
I vowed to fill my mind with as many fascinating ideas and plans
as possible so I would not have to face this emptiness.

Today driving across Massachusetts to collect my son from college,
I watch those same bare limbs etching the borders of the highway,
and the endlessly changing patterns of cars and trucks.
I'm aware of the thin veil that barely separates me from my awkward young self
in the VW bus. I feel like she's sitting next to me now as I drive.

"See with me. This is how I see it now," I say to her.
I feel a wondrous gratitude in how quiet my mind is today.
I find myself in a kind of slow motion,
seeing the rearranging patterns of cars and trees as paintings, studies of light
and color.
Moment by moment, there is that one oak with its twisting arching long branch,
the fans of sumac reaching their red furred seed mounds to the sky,
the yellow glow in the bare willow branches,
the pale red haze in the scrub marsh bushes,
the wide stretching arms of pines, reaching for miles, again and again.
There is a slow simple pleasure now in these highway moments in time.

I look forward to a particular grouping of rust-edged, deep green arbor vitae,
an elegant rearranging Magritte landscape in the green space
between the traffic somewhere between the exit for I-93 and Rt. 2.

My exit appears before I know it, almost effortlessly.
I slip through the maze of city streets and parks finding my son's dorm.
He meets me at the doorway, with a quiet smile of such pleasure.

Our life here in this body is so brief a visit.
I want to treasure every spray of sumac and uprising of oak,
even on the highway, when we are traveling so fast.

Living in the Museum of Snowstorms: Winter Haiku

It's mid-January and still waiting for winter

60-degree wind
feeling the spring in our step
longing for snowstorms

On not knowing what Global Warming has in store for us

welcoming the snow
endangered bird of winter
treasuring what's now

On walking head down into the snow carving drifting winds in early morning months after I forgot to be waiting for the Leaf of Happiness

oak blows me a kiss
mahogany scrap of leaf
snags my scarf and rides

The Friendliness of Snowstorms

"a good foot of snow"
daughter climbs back into bed
a snow day blessing

When my sleepy daughter asks me why I'm so bubbly this winter morning

morning happiness
a poem before breakfast
spices our omelet

Remembering the Fatherlands

Those Garber boys worked on their uncle's horseradish farm
summers in the Ohio Valley, sweat soaking their blond curls,
stinging in their eyes and every breath.
They ate with such voluminous enthusiasm
weighing in before Thanksgiving dinner
to see who could gain the most in one sitting.

Those bald-headed men smoked cigars out on porches on hot summer nights,
the German marching music arching out from the Victrola
into the heavy leafed darkness, flying with the children gathering
fireflies into jars. When the war came, the 78s were broken
and set out with the refuse, and Franz and Friedrich became Fred.

What was German was glossed over by the 50s, sneaking out
only when my father got out that huge copper pot,
big enough to cook all four of his children, to make Bayrische Kartoffeln.
Frying slabs of bacon, sautéing pools of onions turning transparent,
boiling baby red potatoes until their skins split apart,
pouring them all together in that giant pot,
he fed us the flavors of our ancestors with his enthusiasm.

German children in Midwestern towns grew up afraid of Germans.
Nazis pursuing them down the night hallways,
terrified that they might accidentally cross the border
and become the enemy.

Everything was enormous with my father.
His voice exploded the walls when he came into the room.
His enthusiasms vanished my own for decades.
His sun burned so bright I couldn't find my own shadow,
only his. Is every child afraid of their father?

And yet it is the passing of time, the great dilutor of childhood's intensity,
that fades this sunburn, that washes out the sting of horseradish,
for the ease of a diluted life.

On a cold winter night in a whitewashed town at the edge of the North Atlantic,
I see a woman listening to poetry.
We both think for an hour before speaking, that we look familiar,
that we could be cousins. When we speak our names outloud
it is in the forgotten sharp bite of German consonants
that the flavors of our childhoods in Zinzinati come back to us,
like a meal we've yearned for and forgotten.

There's Nothing Like a Flu

There's nothing like a flu to send
a wet sponge wiping across
the blackboard chalked full
with the details of our lives,
leaving us vague and floating.

To reduce our horizons to this bedside collection
of tired water glasses, a litter of tissues,
and the slow flutter of yellow opening,
daffodils in a blue china cup.

To cut the life raft loose,
a bed floating in the center of our world,
only the narrow doorway keeping us
from drifting out into the flurrying snow.

To lose any appetite for the bite and taste
of life, when it takes too much energy to
open our eyes, the lids a heavy coverlet.

To feel my breath inside my body
like a weakly rising tide, careful not
to stir up the crackling of coughs,
the rippling out of aches.

To surrender into hours once filled with appointments,
to forget our mind once filled with desiring,
to take this winter's pause between storms
to curl into this vast emptiness hardly knowing who we are,
to begin practicing how we will let go of this life.

The New Marriage

Years ago, my friend planted a line of pines along the meadow's edge
so that when her daughter married in the full lushness of August
she would walk through an avenue swept with bouquets of white pine boughs
before entering the circle of stones.

Today my snowshoes barely etch the snow.
I take this private avenue as my entryway as well,
accompanied by the unwavering deep tracks of a deer
who traveled this way another day.
Maybe this was my husband I was supposed to meet,
and we've missed each other.
Or maybe this is the new marriage,
entering the circle in the peach light
of a late winter morning
in a day of my own making.

A New Kind of Proposal

I didn't know if I was going to tell you, but
a curious thing happened when I left your house.

Your beautiful old farmhouse, omphalos of your life.
The house at the center of fields, woods circling out beyond.
The house resting at the center of its own valley of quiet,
a stillness you have guarded and lived in all these years.
The old room lit with candles. We sat in front of the wood stove,
spooning more stew out of the fire-blackened pot,
our hair still wet and glistening.
We'd talked in the sauna like old friends do
when lying naked in the dark heat.
You told me of realizing the farm is getting too much for you
to carry all the work alone. You are thinking of building
a little house on the hill.
As I left to drive home in the deep cold night, I stood,
looking up into the sharp-edged stars from the snow-carved path in your yard.

I saw a vision of a possible future for my life opening like a doorway.
I saw myself years ahead living with someone I dearly loved,
talking of poetry and about our day, living here in your house.
I saw myself, your friend and neighbor, as you lived in your little house.
I saw myself being with you as you died.
Further ahead, I saw myself living in that little house as I grew old
and saw myself dying there.
There was no fear, just comfort.
So this is how it could be.

I write you all of this,
And you write back, saying,
Yes, yes to all of it.

The Grant Proposal

Writing a letter at bedtime,
crafting a request for time,
for an empty room full of quiet
where I can listen to what is calling.

I say, I fit poetry in and around
the edges of my life.

The dream writes in its own paragraph.
There is a stream pouring through my house,
a river running under the rug,
diving down between the floorboards,
pushing up with such pressure behind the walls
that it pours out over the crown molding,
cascading down the walls.

The Question We Each Carry

I walk to the ocean in the dark on icy streets,
the blue dawn glowing in every drift,
wondering if I fell, who would find me.

Coming back up the hill a little later,
an ambulance blinks silent amber
a block from my home.
A blanketed figure is guernied to its open arms,
accompanied by the good older men
wrenched from their morning coffee,
who answer the call whenever it comes.

There will be that moment,
when we face the crushing in our chest,
or turn to face the wave,
when we answer our long carried question.
Oh, this is how it will be.

The Best Ex-Husband You Could Ever Ask For

Traveling with my Ex,
we take our daughter and her friend to New York City.
Since we were traveling the same way,
it only made sense.

We settle into an old comfort,
the familiarity of all the years of car trips with our children,
as the girls chatter away in the backseat.
We worry about our sleep-deprived son at college,
and share our amazement at his last paper
he'd emailed both of us for our editing comments.

It's been six years of unwinding the knotted battles,
until they've mostly vanished, forgotten.
What were those battles all about,
when it felt like I was fighting for my life?

He talks of his girlfriend,
of living without making plans.
 I gently hold him at a distance,
as he continues to vaguely court me.
as he, perhaps, vaguely courts all women.
We drive, facing our unknown lives ahead,
wondering about what still waits to be lived.

Mid trip, my mind goes blank with his talk
in all the old familiar ways.
This used to feel like dying, again and again.
Today it's like being a tourist
at a historic battleground.
Grass has grown over all the bloodshed.

We settle into the easy silence
of long married couples,
smiling as we overhear the conversations from the backseat.

It is good to find peace.
No furious expectations haunt us,
no heartbreaking slights,
no land-mined conversations.

We are thoughtful about simple things.
Thank you for driving,
for packing food, for trading off on paying tolls,
for finding this great Salsa club in Soho for our teenaged daughter.

We sit together, the parents, smiling and slightly anxious
as a man asks our daughter to dance.
We stand up as well, but tentatively,
following a rhythm and steps we don't know,
dancing like chaste old friends.
We are careful,
discovering this new dance.

It is Important to Forget

It is important
for winter to be long enough
so that we completely forget the color green.
It is important to forget the smell of earth,
to forget the names of the perennials in our garden,
to forget the sound of birds in the early morning,
to forget the feel of warm breezes across our skin.

It is important for the winter to scour us so thoroughly,
that our gratitude for spring becomes so strong
that we walk evermore steadily into the delight of this day.

It is important
for this absence of love to be long enough,
so that we completely forget what it is to be in love.
It is important to forget lying in bed just touching for hours,
to forget lighting up when our love arrives at our door,
to forget disappearing into kissing while waiting for the teakettle to heat,
to forget what it is to be held all night.

It is important that the absence of love scours us so thoroughly
 that our gratitude for love becomes so strong,
(whether being in love comes to us again or not in this life),
that we walk evermore steadily into the miracle of this day.

The Morning My Inner Dog Woke Me Up

After the long delicious winter's sleep,
the snow up to my window's edge tucking us in,
my inner dog bolts us awake at 5:30 a.m.
on the Ides of March, smelling the ocean.

Nose high in the air,
we hurtle out the door.
No matter there's a fresh coat of snow,
it's all the more enticing.

Closer to the water, other tracks start appearing,
steady boot tracks surrounded by a cacophony of paw prints.
My inner dog travels light,
leaves no tracks and
keeps pulling on the leash.

We clamber over the high tide crusts of salted snow
and hit the beach that's ice-locked us out all winter.
Each step a heavenly sinking into soft yielding sand,
then a pushing off, sink, step, sink, step,
over and over, remembering the give of earth.

The mild tempest of snow strokes the low rocky cliffs,
delicate white etching over dark basalt,
our coast's familiar profile coming back to us
as we trace it with our steps.

My inner dog, so happy as we walk along our summer boulders,
if I could lift my hind leg and pee, I would.

Winter Takes Its Toll

Winter takes its toll.
Spring brings it all to light.

The high tide line is littered with the heavy wreckage of this winter.
In town, the pot dealer for twenty years stumbles along,
his left side limp, stroke bewildered.
The old man who mutters at the center of town all summer
grows older, sits down now, the lines deepening in his haunted face.
I watch the tide of diminishing strength in my aging friends,
the old gardeners' backs arch closer to their gardens.

I start to feel the gaining gravity in the effort to get out of bed,
the contracting of sleep, the need to stretch again into each morning,
the beginning of effort to rise,
to begin again each day,
to have the energy to rise up with the spring
to face another year ahead.

I begin to understand
the slow journey out of this body,
the journey it takes to lose our mooring to this anchorage.

The Smell of Wildness

I once treated a sinewy lone wolf of a Spaniard.
Eyes wide open, shocked like a wild animal,
from the bite of the needle,
"Es muy fuerte," very strong, he growled.
A little afraid, I stood, feeling his pulses
surge below my fingers,
a river I've never followed.
He does not smell American.
He smells like an old wildness
we should not have forgotten.

He knows how to disappear into the hills
and survive when the devouring hordes
come down from the north.
They keep coming century after century.
Burning the villages, starving the people,
inventing new ways to leave the earth barren.
You will know they have arrived when
they legalize their pleasure for torture,
when they shatter and burn whoever will not surrender.
The suits of the cruelest richest pirates to ever plunder
the seven seas gleam like skyscrapers,
as they complete their bloodless coup.
And the Americans smell nothing.

The Seduction

I was easy to seduce, just like my mom.
I just followed the story she'd told me.
The vivid details of the story from my childhood,
how he'd put that vacuum cleaner on her bed,
sucking so much dirt out of her mattress.
Mortified and inspired,
she bought her Kirby.
It was the dirt in the mattress that got me too,
leaving me feeling like a real grown-up,
proudly grasping the upright handle of my very own.

Those clean white demonstration filters mounding with grit and dust
after whirring over my rug a few seconds,
the secret world of dirt coming alive before my astounded eyes.
In a life where I normally can't figure out when to get around to cleaning,
suddenly all I wanted to be doing was vacuuming my house,
our beds, our pillows, pulling out just the right attachment.
There's the spikey edged one for cat hair on the couch,
the long narrow one with the handy removable tiny brush
for those hard-to-reach winter collections of dirt on window ledges.
I start imagining the pleasure of searching out those deep cracks
between the old wide floorboards.

She puts my so-called good vacuum through its paces.
Standing confident in her snazzy heels, moving it
120 times over the same spot, the equivalent
of six months of vacuuming, in an imaginary world I can't imagine.
Then the Kirby glides in, drawing the hidden demons
out of that rug.

How amazing to have a job where you carry
the answer to every problem,
the solution to every challenge,
the tool that will outshine all others,
always taking the prize.
That rug becomes a hidden world of sharp-edged sand
tearing away at the fibers. The mattress is suddenly populated with
mites devouring my dead skin cells as they double the weight
of my bed in ten years.
The immense unsolvable issues of the world suddenly
coalesce in the vastness of the dirt in my house,
that can be met and resolved with such a sleek unstoppable
unbreakable lifetime of astounding engineering,
this magnificent Kirby.

How could I resist? How could I ever
sit on that couch again knowing what lingers there?
How could I ever settle into my bed
happy in my ignorance?
A little knowledge is dangerous,
kidnapping my mind,
my desire completely captivated
with the allure,
the seduction
of vacuuming.

I couldn't wait to call my mom!

Bertha: A Story That Followed Me Home

I was just worn out, about as worn out as I've ever been
and I've had energy to burn my whole life.
My supervisor even noticed and that's amazing
since where I work everyone is worn out.
She said, "Take a week off and get a rest."
So I bought myself a plane ticket to Florida.
I asked my ex if I could stay in his mom's old house,
vacant since she'd died in the fall.

First morning, there I was pulling out the kitchen table
so I could see the back yard.
Clear as a bell, I hear Bertha behind me say,
"Why are you moving my kitchen table?"
Well, I turned around and there she was,
just as real as you and me. And I said, "Bertha!"
And she said, "You can see me?"
"Well," I said, "Not only that, I can hear you too!"

Well, I'd gone for a break from taking care of people,
and wouldn't you know it, the week was spent taking care of Bertha.
She'd gone into the hospital for some kind of test,
and died so fast. She still didn't know she was dead.
It took a long time to convince her.
She said she saw this light open up,
but she didn't realize she was supposed to go to it.
Then it closed down and she's been back here ever since,
confused, trying to figure it out.

First, no one was around. She couldn't understand where everybody
had gone. They'd shipped her body north for the funeral but she didn't
have any use for that body anymore. Next thing she knows there's that
lousy son that said he'd put her in a nursing home if he heard
any more complaints out of her.
So she hadn't said a word, not one for that last 6 months. And there he was
barging into her house, and pawing through her jewelry first thing,
saying who wanted what, and then he was gone too. And I've been
here alone all this time. It's just that no one seems to see me anymore.

Mainly, what she wanted was to talk.
She just needed to have someone
hear how bad those last six months had been.
Sometimes I'd take a break and put the lawn chair
out in that postage stamp of a backyard
and lie in the sun for awhile.
Later she wanted to hear the old songs,

and I sang her all I could remember.
We got out the old records, and played her favorites.
Last time I saw her she was dancing with old Edwin.
He'd showed up by then,
and they were dancing around the living room.
Why, she was just beautiful in a long flowing dress
with her hair twirling around her as she turned.
That was the last I saw her, they just danced off.

Then I went out into that backyard,
to lie in the sun a little until it was time to come home.
She'd said to take whatever clothes I wanted,
so look, isn't this a great pair of pants I got from Bertha?

For Some Reason

For some reason,
when my brothers and I were cleaning
out my father's apartment after he died,
I kept the ribbon-tied mound of letters
my parents had written to each other
when she was 21 and he was 39.

For some reason,
he had kept them all these years, even
after their violent battle of a divorce.

For some reason,
I kept them under my bed for another ten years,
and for some reason, on this raw spring day,
I take them to my mother in her 75th year.

Her first impulse is to burn them immediately.
But then out of curiosity, she begins to read a few
before feeding them to the woodstove in her warm kitchen.
She finds embarrassing her misspelled naive passion,
her small cramped handwriting,
his large expansive handwriting,
her simple life away at college writing nearly daily.
She keeps reading and tossing, stoking the fire.
She pauses, observing with a curious detachment,
as if this has just come to her.
"I guess he was the love of my life."

Then it's time to walk the dogs,
heat up the lamb stew and add the dumplings.
Enjoying our rare quiet evening's visit,
we watch an old BBC Miss Marple mystery.

Later, I fall asleep in the contentment of a child
who has always needed to know, without a doubt,
that at one time, her parents loved each other.

Crush

For years I was famous among my friends for my crushes.
Now I fall the hardest for my newest poem.

There's nothing like waking up with a new poem.
The lines emerging out of sleep,
grabbing my laptop, leaning into my pillows,
catching the words as they leap together
in this new captivating dance,
as the morning light pours through
the lace curtains onto my bed.

And I am so smitten.
I read and reread the words over and over,
and find them marvelous,
sleek, fascinating, perfect just as they settled into place.

But in the next day's less rosy morning light,
the once wondrous phrases stretch too long,
awkward when read out loud.
My dearest friend emails back,
"What did you love so much about this one?"
Oh, no, embarrassed and humbled once again.

I have to head into this poem with my favorite
Japanese Bonsai pruning shears,
and see if I can turn this crush
into a long-term friend.

Listening Inside the Dance

"...and if this teeming Buenos Aires is no more than a dream made up by souls in a common act of magic...."

— JORGE LUIS BORGES

In gratitude to my first teachers of Tango,
Marcela Trapé and Alicia Pons,
and to my remarkable gifted translator.

I chose to have the poems in this section translated into Argentine Spanish (Castellano) to honor the generosity and richness of spirit that we experienced so steadily in Buenos Aires.

Escuchando la Danza

Translations by Demian Gawianski

"…y si esta numerosa Buenos Aires no es más que un sueño
que erigen en compartida magia las almas…."
— JORGE LUIS BORGES

To Cintia, whose sense of poetry helped my
translations become real poems in Spanish

*Elegí acompañar los poemas de esta sección con su traducción
al castellano argentino para honrar la generosidad y la riqueza
espiritual que experimentamos continuamente en Buenos Aires.*

NOTE:
*In order to read these poems with an Argentine Spanish
pronunciation, pronounce the letter "y" in a consonantal
position and the "ll" like the English "sh" sound in "show".
(ie. Mayo sounds like "masho", and ella like "esha")
Also, when preceding another consonant the "s" is
aspirated like the English "h" in "house".*

The Night Plane to Buenos Aires

The moment we step into that sea of faces
we know the climate has changed.
It was as if someone has turned the volume up,
on aliveness,
on vibrancy in the eyes.
Face after face looking into us
A warmth suffusing the air
An air of such personality
Even before we get to our seats,
I am already wondering,
Who would I have been
if I'd been born into this culture?

I sink into my seat,
my heart pounding.

El Avión Nocturno a Buenos Aires

Desde el momento en que pisamos ese mar de rostros
sabemos que el clima ha cambiado.
Como si alguien hubiera subido el volumen,
hacia la vida,
hacia el refulgir de los ojos.
Uno y otro rostro mirándonos
una calidez que sofoca el aire
un aire con personalidad.
Aún antes de llegar a nuestros asientos,
me voy preguntando
¿Quién sería yo
si hubiera nacido en esta cultura?

Tomo asiento,
con el corazón galopante.

A Man Awake

Awakening to a silent crowd of shrouded bodies
sleeping all around me,
I see five seats away,
in a tiny island of light,
a man reading through this long night
as we fly along the spine of the Andes,
the endless birthing of the Amazon
moving out below us.

The man sits sideways,
curled in such comfort,
as if in the couch of his living room,
his hands cradling his book.
His face is finely lined with a warm intelligence
focused in deep concentration.
His hands sometimes touch fingertips under his chin,
sometimes one hand strokes below his lip
after turning a page.

His striking profile,
his absorption,
the pleasure in his fascination,
this man reading in a tiny island of light
surrounded by hundreds hunched over in sleep
in the roar and trembling sea of sound.

He looks like the man
I've wanted to watch reading late at night
my whole life.
Even though he's five seats away
and he wears a gold ring,
that has nothing to do with it.

There is something here
I've always been looking for.
It is enough to watch him read
through the night.

Un Hombre Despierto

Despertando a una silenciosa multitud en penumbras
que duerme a mi alrededor,
veo a cinco asientos,
en una pequeña isla de luz,
a un hombre leyendo en la larga noche
mientras volamos por la espina de los Andes,
el inagotable nacimiento del Amazonas
que se pierde bajo nosotros.

El hombre se recuesta,
se inclina con tal comodidad,
como si estuviera en el sillón de su living,
con sus manos arropando el libro.
Su rostro con los sutiles pliegues de una tibia inteligencia
inmerso en su profunda concentración.
Sus manos rozan a veces el mentón,
a veces una mano se pasea bajo sus labios
luego de cambiar de página.

Su grave perfil,
su absorción,
el placer de su fascinación,
este hombre leyendo en una pequeña isla de luz
rodeado de una muchedumbre que se arquea en su sueño
en el mar furioso del sonido.

Lector en la noche,
parece ser el aquel
que he deseado contemplar toda mi vida.
Los cinco asientos
y su anillo de oro
nada tienen que ver.

Hay aquí algo
que siempre he buscado.
Me basta con verlo leer
a través de la noche.

Buenos Aires

Enormous swirling roaring city
Tearing around every corner
Rivers of taxis pour through the lanes
Filling every avenida with sound.
Diesel exhaust mixes with
Roasting meat and coffee
Entwining with the strains of tango or Madonna
Out of every taxi window.

Billboards sprawling across elegant facades,
Balconies, and shuttered windows,
Patterns of carved stone rippling
From another century.

Settle down past the roar
Discover the islands of tranquility.
Discover vast spaces of quiet
Where time is taken, generously
To face each other in conversation
In long animated vibrant leaning in
Talking in fascination
No one is racing off in a hurry
There is a settling in, to talk
Over tiny cups of coffee, a tiny glass of water,
And pastries on the side
As the later afternoon light turns golden.

When the night settles in
The city comes even more alive
Every shop window glowing with light,
Radiant sheen of fabrics
Cascades of chocolates
Caves lined with books
Crowds of elegant shoes
Night lit faces flowing through it all

As the night deepens, quiets,
Certain closed doors open
Leading to the islands of polished floor
Where the haunting bandoneón
And strings play the songs of the 30s,
Couples dancing in such concentration
Leaning into each other
Heads touching

Eyes closed, listening deeply
Feet etching the golden floor
As the dance is created newly
Again and again
Every night…

There is something here
I've missed my whole life.

NOTE:

Argentine Tango is known worldwide as a dramatic dance with many elaborate movements of the legs and a pre-established choreography. But this is not the way to dance in a "milonga" (tango dancing salon), where couples do not have much space and must follow a direction (opposite to the hands of a clock). This dancing is not addressed to an audience. Its main purpose is establishing a communication with the partner, which comes less from particular steps but from a contact made with the music and in the embrace.

Buenos Aires

Enorme y rugiente torbellino urbano
Que se desgarra en cada esquina.
Ríos de taxis inundan los carriles
llenando cada avenida de sonido.
Los motores confunden sus deshechos
Con la carne asada y el café
Se funden con el tango y con Madonna,
Desde el interior de los taxis.

Carteles que esconden elegantes fachadas,
Balcones, ventanas,
Frisos tallados que se propagan
Desde otro siglo.

Intervalo en el estruendo
Son las islas de la tranquilidad
Vastos espacios para la quietud
Donde el tiempo es tomado generosamente
Para entablar con el otro
Una animada conversación que nos acerca
Hablando con fascinación
Nadie está apurado
Nos disponemos a charlar
Con el vasito de agua y los cafecitos
Las masitas sobre la mesa
Mientras la tarde se vuelve dorada

Cuando la noche se asienta
La ciudad se revitaliza aún más
Las vidrieras radiantes de luz
Un resplandor de fábricas
Cascadas de chocolates
Cuevas alineadas de libros
Una multitud de zapatos elegantes
La iluminada noche lo enfrenta todo en su fluir

Mientras la noche se adentra, se detiene,
Algunas puertas cerradas se abren
Conduciéndonos a las islas de encerado suelo
Donde el lastimero bandoneón
Y las cuerdas tocan temas de los años treinta,
Parejas inclinadas
Bailan en mutua concentración
Cabezas que se tocan

Ojos cerrados, escuchando con atención
Pasos que surcan el salón
A medida que la danza se renueva
Una y otra vez
Noche tras noche...

Hay algo aquí
Que he añorado toda mi vida.

Ode to Dulce de Leche

You were waiting for us
in the cool freshness of Alcira's kitchen,
waiting for her to ask
my travel-wilted daughter,
"Do you like Dulce de Leche?"

From then on mornings became
a vehicle for you,
crisp cut apples sank into your
thick swirl of caramel,
plates of sliced bananas
were side swiped with
rivers of your stickiness,
grapes were smothered
exploding their sour taut bodies
in the bite of your lava of sweetness.
Thin crepes formed in the skillet,
buttered with your thickness,
rolled up warm,
each bite
sinking into your sweetness.

This milk of the pampas
stirred with vanilla and sugar
heated for hours in great copper pots,
thickening and stirring,
thickening into this
heavy swirl of caramel,
the concentrated goodness of milk.
This sticky sweetness, dulce,
where the Argentine children find home.

We carried with us
from the far north,
the thin wild essence,
gathered in buckets,
hauled by Percheron draft horses
to the great cauldron,
boiled for days
watched over by the tall good man
creating our dulce de maple
for Alcira to put on pancakes
for her grandson.

And we carried you home, weighed down
with so many containers of your goodness.
When the customs man asked
"Do you have any food items?"
We asked him,
"Have you ever heard of Dulce de Leche?"
He smiled and waved us through.

Oda al Dulce de Leche

Nos esperabas
en la fresca cocina de Alcira,
cuando ella le preguntó a mi hija
tras su viaje agotador:
"¿Te gusta el dulce de leche?"

En adelante
las mañanas fueron tu vehículo,
trozos de manzana se derramaban
en tu espeso torbellino de caramelo,
platos de bananas trozadas
acogían el peso
de tus adherentes ríos,
las uvas sofocaban
la acidez de sus cuerpos tiesos
al morder tu lava de dulzura.
Hojas de panqueques formadas en la sartén,
al untarse de tu espesura,
se arrollaban calientes,
dejando que cada bocado
se hundiera en tu dulzura.

Esta leche que se revuelve en las Pampas
con vainilla y con azúcar,
que las horas calientan en una gran olla de cobre,
espesándose y revolviéndose,
espesándose hasta devenir
este denso torbellino de caramelo,
la bondad concentrada de la leche.
Es en este pegajoso dulce,
donde los chicos argentinos encuentran su hogar.

Habíamos llevado,
desde nuestro lejano norte,
la esencia fina y salvaje,
condensada en cubetas
y transportada por caballos percherones
hacia la gran caldera,
hervida durante días enteros
y vigilada por el buen hombre
que crea nuestra dulce miel de maple,
con la que Alcira untaría panqueques
para su nieto.

Y te trajimos a casa, en numerosos recipientes
que contuvieron tu bondad.
Cuando el hombre de la aduana nos preguntó
"¿Llevan comida en el equipaje?"
Le replicamos
"¿Escuchó hablar del dulce de leche?"
Sonrió y nos dejó pasar.

First Lesson with Eladia at El Beso

Petite voluptuous swirl of a woman in black,
Looking up at me, she asks,
"You have never danced Close Embrace?"

"You join here," clasping her hand to her bosom,
"Breast to breast,
As one body,
With four legs."

"Hug Me!
You must not be shy!
Wait! Listen inside
To when he moves,
And follow him."

Note:

Close Embrace or Baile milonguero o apilado :
This "milonguero" style is related to the older style of salon Tango dancing. They hold a very close embrace with their straight bodies subtly leaned forward, in order to improve the communication between the couple. This position is also called "apilado" dancing, meaning literally "piled".

Primera Clase con Eladia en El Beso

Arrolladora voluptuosidad de una pequeña mujer vestida de negro
Levantando la mirada, me pregunta
"¿Nunca bailaste apilado?"

"Vení, acércate", sus dedos me llaman, arqueados
"Pecho contra pecho,
como un cuerpo
con cuatro piernas."

"¡Abrazáme!
¡No seas tímida! ¡Esperá!
Escúchalo,
sentí sus movimientos
y seguílo."

The Voices in Your Ear in the Beginning Class

Uno, dos y tres y uno, dos y tres.

Keep your legs close together.
Brush your heels together.

Do not lean back.

Do not be afraid of the man.

No, do not lean down.
Do not hang on the man.

Relax your arms.
Lift your chest.

Uno, dos y tres y uno, dos y tres.

Do not take such long steps.

Stand on your axis, not too forward,
Not too back.

Feet together.
Move your feet in two tracks,
Close together.

Weight all on one foot,
Then the other,
Not halfway one or the other.

Uno, dos y tres y uno, dos y tres.

Do not bend forward.
Do not lean.

Even if he is much shorter,
Stand like a queen.

Uno, dos y tres y uno, dos y tres.

Las Voces que se Oyen en la Primera Clase

Uno, dos y tres y uno, dos y tres.

Mantené las piernas juntas.
Que tus tobillos se rocen.

No te inclines hacia atrás.

No le tengas miedo al hombre.

No, no te agaches.
No te cuelgues del hombre.

Relajá los brazos.
Elevá el pecho.

Uno, dos y tres y uno, dos y tres.

No des pasos tan largos.

Mantenéte sobre tu eje, no muy adelante,
ni demasiado atrás.

Juntá los pies.
Movélos en dos carriles,
pero bien juntos.

Cargá todo el peso sobre un pie,
luego sobre el otro,
nunca entre los dos.

Uno, dos y tres y uno, dos y tres.

No te vayas hacia delante,
no te inclines.

Aunque él sea mucho más bajo,
eleváte como una reina.

Uno, dos y tres y uno, dos y tres.

Being a Beginner

You forget what it's like to be such a beginner,
Learning to walk as if you have never walked.

To forget you have ever mastered anything.
To be so at the beginning.

I watch the grandmother Alcira with her three year old grandson, Augustin,
Telling him over and over as he places magnets on the refrigerator,
Gently, slowly, despacio,
He smashes them on, over and over, and they fall or pop off.
She says it again and again, and his style slowly changes.
More carefully, slower, he moves them into place,
Until they are all on.
Then he takes them all off and begins again.

I am a three year old all over again,
In not knowing,
A relief in not knowing,
Being told again and again,
How to begin to walk,
How to listen through the body,
How to step outside of knowing,
To step into this opening,
Having only to be open.

Ser Principiante

Uno se olvida de lo que es ser un verdadero principiante,
aprendiendo a caminar como si uno nunca hubiera caminado.

Olvidar que uno ha sabido hacer algo alguna vez.
Ser tan principiante.

Veo a la abuela Alcira con su nieto de tres años, Agustín,
diciéndole una y otra vez mientras él coloca imanes en la heladera,
"tranquilo, despacio",
al tiempo que, una y otra vez, los tira con fuerza, resbalan y se caen.
Ella se lo repite y el estilo del chico cambia levemente.
Más despacio y con un poco más de cuidado, los ubica en el lugar,
hasta que todos se hallan colocados.
Luego los desprende y vuelve a empezar.

Yo vuelvo a ser una niña de tres años,
en el no saber,
en el sosiego del no saber,
mientras me indican y me repiten,
cómo empezar a caminar,
cómo escuchar con el cuerpo,
cómo salirme del conocimiento,
ubicarme en la apertura,
con el solo deber de estar abierta.

Generosity

The man looks like a gentle Neruda,
plaid shirt and khakis.
in the kindness of his 60s.
He says, "This is how we touch."
as he pats the side of his forehead
and mine. And we lean into the embrace.

He says, "You stand and lean forward,
in a straight line, from your big toes.
You practice this every day, all day,
from now on."

He leads me patiently,
practicing stepping back,
encircling the floor.
He coaxes simply, saying, "Force, mas force,
with each step. Force, force,
Si, muy bien, force, step, force."
Through song after song,
saying force, force when my step weakens,
Until the series is over, and he graciously bows.

Later I watch him dancing with a lovely young woman.
Her feet so delicate, like gentle birds playing
behind her. He leads so clearly,
his eyes closed, his face warm with pleasure.

Later, as he prepares to leave,
he comes to me in generosity,
and dances his last dance with me.
Leading me again, to practice, walking backward.
Step by step, his voice leading,
force, with each step, force, quietly in my ear.
Forehead to forehead, chest to chest
With my Neruda man.
grateful for such kindness,
leading me in my beginning steps,
over and over.
Finishing he says, "Muy bien,
así está mejor.".Much better.

Generosidad

El hombre parece un gentil Neruda
con su camisa a cuadros y su pantalón verde
en la bondad de sus sesenta años.
"Así es como establecemos contacto", me dice
al palmear con suavidad su frente
y la mía. Y nos entregamos al abrazo.

Me dice: "Vos inclínate hacia delante,
en una línea recta que nace de la punta de tus pies.
Practicá esto todos los días, todo el día,
de hoy en adelante."

Conduce con paciencia
mis pasos hacia atrás,
imprimiendo curvas en el suelo.
Me persuade con simpleza: "Fuerza, más fuerza,
en cada paso. Fuerza, fuerza,
Sí, muy bien, fuerza, un paso más, fuerza."
Me va pidiendo fuerza, a través de las canciones,
fuerza cuando mi paso se debilita,
hasta el final del baile. Luego inclina ante mí toda su gracia.

Más tarde lo veo bailar con una hermosa bailarina,
sus pies tan delicados, su baile como pájaros
que juegan detrás de ella. Él la conduce con claridad,
con los ojos cerrados, y la cara templada de placer.

Más tarde, mientras prepara su partida,
me acerca toda su generosidad
y baila conmigo la última pieza.
Me conduce en una nueva práctica, hacia atrás.
Paso tras paso, su voz me guía,
fuerza, a cada paso, fuerza, suave en mi oído.
Frente contra frente, pecho contra pecho
con mi Neruda.
Agradecida por esta amabilidad
que guía mis primeros pasos
una y otra vez.
Al terminar me dice: "Muy bien,
así está mejor". Mucho mejor.

Waiting for my teacher

Pausing,
Watching from outside,
Pausing,
Waiting for days,
Watching the teachers in their studios,
Students following steps
Turning, feet leading, following,
I keep listening,
Waiting.
Who can help me enter this dance?
Patient,
Scared,
Frustrated,
Tired,
Scared,
Determined.

Waiting.
Deciding to keep waiting,
Trusting,
Watching the dancers in
The embrace of light,
Circling
Over well-worn floors.

How to enter
This life in the body.
How to begin
This surrender into listening.
Pausing before beginning.
Knowing it is to step
Off the edge
Into another life.

Pausing,
Waiting,
Preparing,
Readying.

Esperando a Mi Maestro

Una pausa,
mirando desde afuera,
una pausa,
espera interminable.
Miro a los profesores en los salones
y a los estudiantes que imitan sus pasos,
haciendo giros, guiados por sus pies, imitando.
Yo sigo escuchando,
esperando.
¿Quién puede ayudarme a penetrar en esta danza?
Paciente,
temerosa,
frustrada,
cansada,
temerosa,
decidida.

Espero,
decido seguir esperando,
confío,
mirando a los bailarines
abrazados por la luz,
dando vueltas
sobre pistas desgastadas.

Cómo introducir
esta vida en el cuerpo.
Cómo encarar
la sumisión al sonido.
Deteniéndome antes de empezar.
Dando un primer paso
más allá de mis límites
hacia una nueva vida.

Una pausa,
espero,
me preparo,
estoy lista.

My Daughter at the Milonga

Six months before, my fourteen-year-old daughter had said,
"I want to learn Argentine Tango more than anything in the world."
Amazed, I answer, "Really? Well, I think that's the kind of thing
you do when you are in college."
But that line of hers stayed with me,
working under the current of my days.

Now I find myself at the crowded edge at El Beso,
in the midnight smoky blue haze of this cozy small dance club.
The dance floor is packed with men, dapper in low double-breasted suits,
and the women sleek, bare backs criss-crossed with thin straps,
flowing legs in silk, feet adorned in jewels of handmade shoes.

My daughter is ready to dance. Stately and graceful beyond her years,
three years of ballroom dance make her facile and quick with new steps.
Relaxing out of the rigid arching back frame of American tango,
she has softened into this very different stance,
stepping cautiously into this first night to dance in close embrace.

We've been coached in the dance of eyes that mark an invitation to dance.
She says, "It's so funny, Mom. In the States, if you like someone you don't
look at them. Here I just look around and people are looking at me."
She kept looking back down for awhile, and then with a friend,
they stood up together, eyes softly open, glancing slowly about,
available, ready to dance.

The first man catches her eye, comes up
bowing his head slightly. She glances back a moment at me,
and then they are off to the floor, entering the slow moving circling
of bodies dissolved into an architecture of movement.
I see her for moments through the figures.
Her hair glinting golden, her face uplifted,
her skirt twirling as she turns and follows.
They pause between dances. She chats in Spanish,
saying she's from a little town of 6,000 in Neuva Inglaterra,
before they dance again, until the series is over,
when she is returned to me.

Each next dancer who invites her to dance is better,
a better leader, and she likes the last best.
She says he reminds her of her dad.
Then it's time for my big girl and me
to walk home arm in arm to our room.
She leans against me at bedtime,

asks me to brush her long hair.
We lie down in our twin beds to sleep.
"Night, night, mommy. Thank you so much."
"Good night, sweetheart."

Mi Hija en la Milonga

Seis meses atrás, mi hija de catorce años había dicho:
"Quiero aprender a bailar tango argentino más que nada en el mundo."
Maravillada, respondí: "¿En serio? Bueno, creo que ése es el tipo de cosas
que una hace cuando está en la facultad."
Pero esa frase suya quedó grabada en mi memoria,
resonando en el fluir de mis días.

Ahora me encuentro en la puerta transitada de El beso,
en la nocturna bruma azul de este salón acogedor.
La pista está concurrida, colmada de apuestos hombres de traje,
y de mujeres distinguidas, tachadas por finos breteles sus espaldas desnudas,
piernas de seda que flotan, pies adornados en joyas de zapatos artesanales.

Mi hija está lista para bailar. Majestuosa y elegante más allá de su edad,
tres años de danza de salón la hicieron dócil a los nuevos pasos.
Descansando de la estructura rígida del tango americano,
se ha ablandado hacia esta postura por completo diferente,
en su cuidadoso ingreso a esta primera noche de baile milonguero.

Habíamos sido ya entrenadas en la danza de los ojos que marca la invitación
a bailar.
Me dice: "Es tan gracioso, mamá. En Estados Unidos, si te gusta alguien
no lo mirás. Acá, doy vuelta la cabeza y la gente me está mirando."
Siguió un rato aún mirando al piso y después, con una amiga,
se pararon juntas y abrieron bien los ojos, registrando con calma a su
alrededor,
disponibles, listas para bailar.

Un primer hombre captura su mirada, se acerca
con una ligera inclinación de cabeza. Ella me dirige una breve mirada,
y ya están en la pista, adentrándose en la lenta circulación,
de cuerpos disueltos en una arquitectura de movimiento.
La veo por momentos entre las figuras.
Su dorado pelo reluciente, su rostro elevado,
la agitada pollera acompañando sus giros.
Se detienen entre dos tangos. Ella charla en castellano,
diciendo que viene de un pequeño pueblo de 6.000 habitantes en Nueva
Inglaterra,
antes de que reanuden su baile, hasta el final de la tanda,
momento en el que vuelve a mí.

Cada bailarín que la saca a bailar es mejor que el anterior,
un mejor conductor, y es siempre el último el que ella prefiere.
Dice que le hace acordar a su papá.

Se hace al fin la hora de que mi gran hija y yo
debamos volver a nuestro cuarto tomadas de los brazos.
A la hora de dormir, ella se inclina ante mí,
pidiéndome que le cepille su largo pelo.
Nos acostamos en nuestras camas para dormir.
"Buenas noches, mami. ¡Y un millón de gracias!"
"Buenas noches, princesa."

Finding My Teacher

Your teacher is the one
Who loves you
Simply because you
Have walked through their door,
Ready and open.

They know that you can dance.
Their knowing opens up the dancer
That has always been waiting to emerge.

They are the stone carver
Waiting for the marble to say
Who is waiting to emerge.

I am being given this gift
I have spent years learning to give.

To awaken the other
In whatever language we've been given
So that we may begin our dance.

Buscando a Mi Maestro

Tu maestro es aquél
Que te quiere
Simplemente
Porque atravesaste su puerta
Listo y predispuesto.

Sabe que podés bailar.
Su conocimiento despierta al bailarín
Que ha estado siempre esperando emerger.

Es la piedra talladora
Que espera a que el mármol le indique
Quién es el que espera emerger.

Un obsequio me está siendo entregado
Que he pasado años aprendiendo a otorgar.

Despertar al otro
En cualquier lenguaje que nos haya sido dado
Para que empecemos a bailar.

The First Teacher
(for Marcela Trapé)

I am sitting in the corner,
Watching my daughter at a lesson,
Carving elegant backwards curving steps,
When Marcela arrives.

She is a tiny delight,
A beam of sparkling eyes,
Her every move,
an adorable leap of flexibility.

She leans forward,
Kissing me on the cheek,
Really asking, her warmth a balm,
"How was your day today?"

And I realize this is who
I want to learn from.

I return for the lesson shyly.
Stepping out of the city's roar
Into this still room,
Billows of fabric softening the ceiling,
Wall of mirrors, blond floor ready.

She has a lambskin for me in the center of the floor.
She says, "This dance is not hard, or difficult.
It is just walking, forward and back. It is no big deal!"
Her face so delightful, her knowing so sure,
That I step into her knowing.

"But you cannot just walk off the street and begin.
You have to release the body first."
I lie down, and feel the pressures of traveling,
of speaking another language,
of all the decisions,
of being a tired mother,
Relaxing.
I go still and quiet in her tenderness.

She begins the release,
Gently circling my wrist, then my elbow,
Turning and moving my shoulder
From the tight hold of carrying the world.

La Primera Profesora
(para Marcela Trapé)

Estoy sentada en el rincón,
Mirando a mi hija en la clase
Tallar elegantes pasos curvos hacia atrás,
Cuando llega Marcela.

Es una pequeña delicia
Un haz de ojos resplandecientes
Cada movimiento suyo,
un adorable brote de flexibilidad.

Se inclina hacia delante
Besándome en la mejilla,
Con su calidez de bálsamo que me pregunta de verdad:
"¿Cómo fue tu día hoy?"

Y me doy cuenta de que es ella
De quien quiero aprender.

Vuelvo a tomar la clase, tímida.
Al margen del rugido de la ciudad
En esta apacible habitación,
Paños ondulados que suavizan el cielo raso,
Una pared de espejos, y el dorado piso disponible.

Ella me tiene preparada una alfombra de piel en el centro de la pista.
Me dice: "Este baile no es complicado, ni difícil,
es sólo caminar hacia delante y hacia atrás. ¡No es gran cosa!"
Su cara es tan deliciosa, su conocimiento tan seguro,
Que me sumerjo en su saber.

"Pero no podés simplemente salir a la calle y empezar.
Primero tenés que soltar tu cuerpo."
Me recuesto, y siento la tensión de viajar,
de hablar otra lengua,
de todas las decisiones,
de ser una madre cansada,
Me voy relajando.
Con calma, me voy adentrando en su ternura.

Ella empieza la relajación,
Moviendo mi muñeca en delicados círculos, luego mi codo,
Girando y liberando mi hombro
De la pesada carga de sostener el mundo.

The Panther
(for Alicia Pons)

I let a panther of a woman
take my chest between her hands,
lifting me, demanding of me:
"You have to be alive here!"

Penetrating dark eyes,
Waves of red hair,
A fierce warmth
Commanding me.

"All your energy is here, in your chest!"
As she holds my sides, we begin to walk.
I follow her lead, her eyes,
her hands grasping my ribs so strongly.
"There is no weight in your legs,
It is all up here!"

I feel it!
This rising up into my chest,
and for a moment, my legs feel
as though they could lift off.
Sliding, stepping so easily.
Her knowing so certain,
lifting me out of the myth of gravity,
without me
weighing myself down.

This practice room, this circle of light
above the street, this cave of the world,
with Alicia propelling me into dance.
Touching my upper chest.
"Your power is here."
Pressing her hand strongly onto my sternum.
Her eyes, her breath, so close,
searing into me.
"This is where you communicate,
your passion, your presence.
Chest to chest.
The dance is a dialogue
through your body
with the man."

She is translating into my body a new language,
creating a new life of living in this body.
A life of rising up into another life.
A life not yet lived.
"Be a fountain of water pouring up through you!
A great column of water rising out of your head."

I set sail in a tiny sailing ship,
Setting forth to ride that great column of water,
Not knowing what shore it will take me to.

La Pantera
(para Alicia Pons)

Dejo que una mujer pantera
tome mi pecho entre sus manos,
elevándome, exigiéndome:
"¡Es acá donde tenés que estar viva!"

Penetrantes ojos oscuros,
un cabello rojo ondulado,
una feroz calidez
que me da indicaciones.

"¡Toda tu energía está acá, en el pecho!"
Me toma por los costados y empezamos a caminar.
Sigo su guía, sus ojos,
sus manos que se adhieren con fuerza a mis costillas.
"No hay peso en tus piernas.
¡Está todo acá!"

¡Y yo siento
esto que escala hasta mi pecho!
Y mis piernas sienten, por un momento,
como si pudieran despegar.
Me deslizo, mis pies se desplazan con facilidad.
Su conocimiento tan certero
me eleva por sobre el mito de la gravedad,
evitando que yo misma
me obligue a caer.

Este salón de baile, este círculo de luz
sobre la calle, esta cueva del mundo,
con Alicia impulsándome a bailar.
Toca la parte superior de mi pecho.
"Tu poder está acá."
Presiona su mano sobre mi esternón.
Sus ojos, su aliento, tan cerca,
agotándose ante mí.
"Acá es donde comunicás
tu pasión, tu presencia.
Pecho contra pecho.
La danza es un diálogo
con el hombre
a través de tu cuerpo."

Ella está traduciendo una nueva lengua al lenguaje de mi cuerpo,
creándole a este cuerpo una nueva vida.
Una vida como un despertar en otra vida
Una vida no vivida aún.

Me hago al mar en una pequeña embarcación,
y procuro timonear esa columna de agua,
ignorando la orilla en la que he de recalar.

Making "The Cross"

Her body moves as one fluid wave.
Time slows down, moment by moment,
watching the simplest act
of one foot crossing over the other.
Her foot points, arches slowly, rises,
carrying through the air,
etches the ground, pausing to collect,
before sliding up and around,
crossing the other foot,
slipping into position delicately,
slowly articulating the unfolding of her panther's
foot to the touch of earth, her weight shifting,
and she pauses there.

All the time in the world pauses for that
moment for one foot to lift, collect and cross.

The painter lifts the brush with just the right color
and slowly lets the brush down on the canvas.
The pianist raises her hand, arching over the keys
before slowly moving down to touch sound.

NOTE:

The Cross (El Cruce) is a step where the woman passes her left foot in front of her right, to finish with her legs crossed and facing the man. It is the fifth step in the eight step basic tango sequence.

Haciendo "El Cruce"

Su cuerpo fluye como un río.
El tiempo, poco a poco, se va deteniendo,
en la contemplación del simple acto
de un pie cruzando sobre el otro.
Su pie se estira, se arquea suavemente, se eleva,
resonando en el aire,
surca el suelo, deteniéndose para recibir
antes de deslizarse en derredor
de cruzar el otro pie
de resbalar con delicadeza hacia su posición
de articular el lento despliegue de su pie de pantera
hacia el contacto con la tierra, momento en que traslada el peso
y se detiene.

Todo el tiempo del mundo se detiene en ese instante,
para que un pie se eleve, reciba al otro y lo cruce.

El pintor levanta el pincel con el color indicado
y lo deja caer preciso sobre el lienzo.
El pianista eleva su mano, la arquea sobre las teclas
luego la deja descender hacia el sonido.

The Smell of an Evening

You carry the night of dancing
home in your hair.
The tangled smells of men and sweat
and bite of smoke.
Swishing your perfumed hair
across your face again and again,
before falling asleep.

A City of Kisses

Every greeting a leaning in to kiss,
Touching cheeks,
Lovers in trees,
On benches in parks,
And we dance at El Beso.

By the time we return the seventh time,
We are being kissed hello.

El Olor de un Atardecer

Te llevás a casa
la noche de baile en el pelo.
Entremezclado el sudor con el olor de los hombres
y un bocado de humo.
Hacés crujir tu perfumado pelo
por tu cara una y otra vez,
hasta dormirte.

Una Ciudad de Besos

Cada saludo es una inclinación al beso
Mejillas que se tocan
Amantes en los árboles
En los bancos de los parques
Y bailamos en El beso.

Nuestra séptima visita
es bienvenida con un beso.

The Conversation We Do Not Have

We never asked anyone,
What was it like thirty years ago
in the time of the Disappeared?
Who did you know?
Where did it happen?

No one asks us, How can you stand it?
To live in the time of the disappearances,
when they are shipped out without names
to Guantanamo, without charges,
without council, held outside of time.

We do not ask what is happening
to those who live with the blood of torture
on their souls who have slipped outside the law?

No one asks us, How can you stand it?
To have your young men and women
initiated into the horrors of torture?
No one asks, Will they be brought to trial,
or live with that horror the rest of their lives?

Only one brilliant vivacious woman asked us
the questions we could not answer.

"What is happening in the States?
Everything we hear is so crazy.
We can't understand it.
We hear that the top scientists in the country
are afraid to teach evolution.
How can people be so afraid?"

"It is obvious to the whole world
that they let 9/11 happen so Bush
could be the big hero
and they could do anything they wanted.
How can Americans be so blind?
When I came to the States in the 70s
it was the beacon of hope for all of us.
How can people be so afraid?"

La Conversación Que No Tenemos

Nunca le preguntamos a nadie:
¿Cómo era vivir hace treinta años
en la época de los desaparecidos?
¿A quiénes conocías?
¿Dónde ocurrió?

Nadie nos pregunta: ¿cómo pueden soportar
vivir en la época de las desapariciones,
cuando son embarcados, sin nombres,
a Guantánamo, sin cargos,
sin defensa, mantenidos fuera del tiempo?

No preguntamos qué les pasa hoy
a los que han ignorado la ley y viven
con la sangre de la tortura en sus almas.

Nadie nos pregunta: ¿Cómo pueden soportar
que sus jóvenes estén
iniciados en los horrores de la tortura?
Nadie pregunta si van a ser llevados a juicio,
o si van a vivir con ese horror por el resto de sus vidas.

Sólo una mujer vivaz
nos hizo las preguntas que no podíamos responder.

"¿Qué está pasando en Estados Unidos?
Lo que escuchamos es tan raro.
No lo podemos entender.
Nos dicen que los mayores científicos del país
tienen miedo de enseñar la teoría de la evolución.
¿Cómo se puede tener tanto miedo?

Es obvio para todo el mundo
que dejaron que los atentados ocurrieran
para convertir a Bush en el gran héroe
y hacer todo lo que quisieran.
¿Cómo pueden ser tan ciegos los americanos?
Cuando yo fui a Estados Unidos en los '70
era la luz de la esperanza para nosotros.
¿Cómo se puede tener tanto miedo?"

Released from Smiling
Discovering the American demand for smiles.

A family has their photo taken, and my daughter
notices they don't smile, they look steadily.

The face relaxes into itself.
The neutral present face,
The face of this moment,
With nothing added,
With nothing expected,
With no complaints,
A face ready to be present,
A strong fully present face,
Moving as part of a whole body,
Gazing with interested attention.
With eyes looking steadily
Into the eyes of the other.

The Relief of Rain

The relief of rain after a week of sun.
The relief of this room in Palermo Viejo,
the quiet cobblestone streets after city traffic.
The relief of the green room with French doors
opening to the balcony, and
the jacaranda tree blossoming its pink cloud.
The relief of the small avenues
of Borges's comforting sycamores,
their quilt of white, green and camel bark
dappling the light of our walks.
The relief of discovering a love affair
worthy of consuming me,
in this dance,
in this city.

Exentos de Sonreír
Descubriendo la necesidad americana de sonrisas.

Vemos la foto de una familia, y mi hija
Observa que no sonríen, parecen serenos.

La cara se relaja en sí misma.
La neutra cara actual,
La cara de este momento,
Sin nada agregado,
Sin expectativas,
Sin quejas,
Una cara lista para estar,
Una cara firme y presente,
Moviéndose más allá del cuerpo,
Fijando la mirada con atención.
Ojos serenos
Que miran al otro a los ojos.

El Alivio de la Lluvia

El alivio de la lluvia tras una semana de sol.
El alivio de este cuarto de Palermo Viejo,
el calmo empedrado tamizando el tráfico urbano.
El alivio verde del cuarto,
de sus puertas francesas que se abren hacia el balcón
y al jacarandá que da brote a su rosada nube.
El alivio de las pequeñas avenidas,
de las Borgeanas higueras sosegadoras,
con su manto verde y blanco, su parda corteza,
salpicando de luz nuestras caminatas.
El alivio de descubrir un amor
capaz de consumirme
en esta danza,
en esta ciudad.

Sunday Afternoon Tango Lesson in the Sala of Our B&B

The lean gray self possessed cat arrives with the dancers.
The tall sweet Belén leans in the doorway,
at 19, she says, "I don't like Tango. It is for the old."
but she wants to see these Americans dance.

Meredith's laptop opens to a vast library of dances.
The dancers begin under the chandelier,
the parquet of the floor moving in patterns under their feet,
the stairway circles up around the borders of the room.

The black lab enters, smelling with interest,
then sprawls out underfoot and has to be dragged away.
The dancers turn and step, learning to change from
leading to following, from mother to daughter to dancers
in the afternoon light through the arched doorway.

The little fire in the embers under the gray marble mantle
takes off the autumn chill, and the dancers turn and step
in the poignancy of strings, clarinet, and bandoneón,
The sound of Buenos Aires moves out through the door
over the polished smooth black and white tiles,
carrying the heavy brass keys that open the wrought iron doorway,
out into the street,
whipping the cascading swirling tiny yellow leaves
blown past the orange wall,
through the black and yellow radio taxi's blanketing the city,
around the polished windows of pastelerías,
past the women washing the sidewalks in front of their shops,
up and circling the white balconied edificios,
out past the tailored sprawl of polo fields,
over the avenidas of trees
until the music joins the Río de la Plata
spreading out like the vast soil-browned sea.

Clase de Tango en la Sala de Nuestro Hospedaje, un Sábado por la Tarde

El flaco gato gris entra con decisión junto a los bailarines.
La dulce Belén se detiene en la puerta.
Con sus 19 años, dice: "No me gusta el tango. Es para los viejos."
Pero quiere ver bailar a estos americanos.

La computadora de Meredith se abre a una vasta biblioteca de danzas.
Bajo la araña de luz, los bailarines dan inicio a su actividad,
desplazando el parquet bajo sus pies,
con la escalera que se alza por las paredes.

Entra el labrador negro, olfateando con interés,
luego se arrellana en el suelo, y es arrastrado hacia fuera.
Los bailarines dan pasos y giros, aprenden a cambiar
del conducir al seguir, de madre a hija a bailarines
en la luz vespertina que ingresa por la arqueada puerta.

El pequeño fuego bajo la camisa gris de mármol
elimina la frialdad, y los bailarines dan pasos y giros
en la conmoción de las cuerdas, el clarinete y el bandoneón.
Este sonido de Buenos Aires huye por la puerta,
flota sobre las pulidas baldosas negras y blancas,
transporta las pesadas llaves de bronce que abren el portal de hierro forjado,
hacia la calle,
azota las pequeñas y revueltas hojas amarillas
que florecen junto a la pared anaranjada,
rumbo a los taxis negros y amarillos que tapizan la ciudad,
atraviesa las limpias ventanas de las pastelerías,
pasa junto a las mujeres que lavan las veredas de sus negocios,
rodea los blancos edificios con balcones,
cruza las improvisadas canchas de polo,
sobre avenidas de árboles
hasta que la música se une al Río de la Plata
esparciéndose como el vasto pardo impuro mar.

Listening Inside the Dance:
(Even Beginners Can Discover Tango Bliss)

disappearing into
this sinuous
luxurious stream
of movement with
eyes closed,
warm forehead
to forehead,
waves of hair
across my cheek,
chest to chest
in close embrace

a lead so fine
the dance
arises,
effortlessly,
naturally,
it's all the body
wants to do
is follow
this flow
of turning
lifting
fluidity
eyes closed
radiant
darkness,
behind
the eyes
glowing,
smiling
radiating
through
every inch
of me.

Escuchando la Danza
(Aún los Principiantes Pueden Descubrir la Dicha del Tango)

Desapareciendo
Hacia esta sinuosa,
Lujuriosa corriente
De movimiento con
Ojos cerrados,
Tibia frente
Contra frente,
Olas de cabello
Tachando mi mejilla,
Pecho contra pecho
En el abrazo

Una fina guía
La danza
Se eleva,
Sin esfuerzo,
Con naturalidad,
Todo lo que el cuerpo
Quiere hacer
Es seguir
Este flujo
De giros
Ascensos
Fluidez
Ojos cerrados
Radiante
Oscuridad,
Detrás
De los ojos
Que brillan
Sonríen
Irradian
A través
De cada parte
De mí.

The Last Morning Before We Leave

I who live to be awake at dawn at home,
laugh when I carry my watch out of the curtained darkness
to see what terrible hour this is to be up and about in the silent house.
Amused, I smile: it's 7 a.m., my old friend.

7 a.m. feels like the middle of the night.
7 a.m. feels like a rude time to be tiptoeing about.
7 a.m. is too early to be up in this city
that goes to bed so late.
7 a.m. is our 3 a.m.
7 a.m. is filled with all these words that bolted me awake,
sending me out to wander in my nightgown
for a place near a lamp to write,
so I may carry this city home with me.

La Mañana Anterior a Nuestra Partida

Yo, que acostumbro estar despierta al amanecer,
me río cuando, al asomar mi reloj tras la cortina,
veo qué terrible hora es para reanudar la rutina en esta casa silenciosa.
Divertida, sonrío: son las 7 de la mañana, amigo mío.

Las 7 parecen la mitad de la noche.
Las 7 no es momento siquiera para andar en puntas de pie.
Las 7 es demasiado temprano para estar despierto
en esta ciudad que tan tarde se va a dormir.
Las 7 de aquí son nuestras 3 de la mañana.
Las 7 son esta lluvia de palabras que me expulsa de la cama,
forzándome a vagar en camisón
en busca de un rincón con luz donde escribir,
y así llevar esta ciudad conmigo.

Bringing the Dance Home

North Atlantic Tango practice

Flying from golden Argentine autumn
to raw Maine spring in one day.
Carrying these voices home,
I step carefully in the sand beside the cold sea.
practicing their steps in my own soil,
to intertwine their dance,
into my landscape,
to imbed it into my walk.

The frigid waves steadily
echo my Neruda man's voice
saying "force, force" in time with the waves.
Alicia calls for this energy to be alive in my chest,
Marcela reminds me to lift my arms from below,
I remember to stay on my axis,
as I practice dancing in this life.

Returning Home to Discover Exile

I can't step easily into my old invisibility.
I can't step back peacefully into the old joys
of my solitary life.

My ocean was my love waiting
for me each morning.
My garden awaited my searching fingers,
my sweat.
My poetry books warmed my bed,
tucking me in every night.
Every luxurious Saturday morning
snuggling into words.

I walked these streets,
enraptured with every detail
of light on well-framed white clapboards
and wood fanning above Federal doorways,
of lavender horizons reflected
in wavery old glass.

My patients reach out their stories to me
and I try to hear into them deeper than anyone
has ever heard them,
so they may heal at last.
My children grasp for my attention,
refilling their well of mother
before they are off
in the absorption of their lives.

How strange that in that city where I was a stranger
I felt so seen as a woman,
and here at home,
I pass like an elegant ghost, unseen.

Traveling Through Cultures of Eyes

I passed through a city where I was seen.
A city of living in the eyes,
a city of presence.
where to look carefully is a developed art,
a slow, thoughtful practice.

There is the good solid warmth of the white-coated waiter
as he brings each course of dishes and heavy white napkins.
Belen's youth smiles her delight into our eyes.
Alcira tells the story from Bergman's last film and our eyes
well up in a long look of recognized grief.
Otilia's eyes pierce mine with her passionate concern,
What is happening to my friend's child?
The grandmother putting on her white scarf at Plaza de Mayo,
where the mothers of the disappeared have kept meeting for thirty years,
returns my honoring look with a long tender sweet smile,
so familiar I remember my grandmother's eyes.
Alicia's eyes catapult a stream of aliveness.
Her eyes suspend time, holding me locked into the dance.
The man with his white shirtsleeves rolled up,
who murmurs gently in English as we dance
meets my eyes with anticipation without intrusion,
in this city where the dance of eyes always precedes the dance.

The journey home is to pass through cultures of eyes.
In D.C., the eyes bore holes in the polished floors,
or ricochet across faces as fast as the clicking heels.
Back in Maine, eyes glance by with a comfortable vagueness.

The loss is stunning.

Just let me find the eyes of the graying curly haired man
who passed by in the Barrancas de Belgrano,
looking with a slow focused intelligence,
without a thread of seduction, just a look of consideration,
a breath of mature presence passing by.
I could live my life with a man who looked at me that way.

But today, it is enough to put on my foul weather gear
and head out into this spring pelting rain
wide eyed, watching everything with my strong gaze.

The black crow walking intently on the brilliant new green.
My beloved oak pregnant with legions of budding leaves.
My bay stoked into storm silvered eruptions.

The roiling ocean of sky
hurtles over my wide open eyes,
receiving all of this.
And every detail of this spring storm
looks right back at me,
straight into my eyes, steady,
and unflinching.

Un Viaje por las Culturas de los Ojos

Viajé a una ciudad donde fui vista.
Una ciudad de ojos vitales,
una ciudad con presencia.
donde mirar con atención es un arte desarrollado,
una práctica lenta y pensativa.

Allí está la calidez del mozo de chaqueta blanca
que trae cada plato con su servilleta de tela.
La juventud de Belén nos sonríe a los ojos.
Alcira cuenta la trama de la última película de Bergman
y mana de nuestros ojos una mirada de aflicción.
Los ojos de Otilia horadan los míos con su apasionada preocupación:
¿Qué le está pasando a la hija de mi amiga?
La abuela, ciñendo su pañuelo blanco en la Plaza de Mayo,
donde las madres de los desaparecidos se siguieron reuniendo durante 30 años,
devuelve mi mirada de admiración con una larga y tierna sonrisa.
Tan cercanos sus ojos como los ojos de mi abuela en mi recuerdo.
Los ojos de Alicia irradian su flujo de vitalidad.
Sus ojos suspenden el tiempo, dejándome sellada a esta danza.
El hombre de camisa blanca arremangada,
que murmura en inglés mientras bailamos,
encuentra mis ojos con anticipación pero sin intrusión.
En esta ciudad donde la danza de los ojos siempre precede a la danza.

En casa, los días consisten en atravesar las culturas de los ojos.
En Washington, los ojos cavan agujeros en el suelo,
o rebotan en las caras de los otros con la misma rapidez de los pasos.
De vuelta en Maine, los ojos se pasean en una cómoda vaguedad.

La pérdida es asombrosa.

Preciso buscar los ojos de aquel hombre de pelo cano y enrulado
que pasó caminando por Barrancas de Belgrano,
mirando con una inteligencia lenta y enfocada,
sin aires de seducción, tan sólo una atenta mirada,
el aliento de una madura presencia que pasa junto a nosotras.
Yo podría vivir toda la vida con un hombre que me mirara de ese modo.

Pero hoy, me basta con asumir este mal tiempo
aceptando esta mezquina lluvia primaveral
con los ojos bien abiertos, observándolo todo con mirada penetrante.

El cuervo negro que camina resuelto sobre el verde prado.
Mi amado roble fecundo en hojas prontas a florecer.

Mi bahía en su tormenta de plateadas erupciones.
El irritante océano del cielo
precipitándose sobre mis ojos abiertos,
recibiéndolo todo,
mientras cada detalle de esta tormenta primaveral
me devuelve una frontal mirada,
directa hacia mis ojos, firme,
y resuelta.

Rediscovering Myself in Borges' Dream, Again and Again

One thing that regularly pried my mother out
of the grip of our childhood was her Monday Class
group of women who studied the literature of a culture
a year at a time. The year they studied Russian fiction
my mother made a map of Russia as big
as our dining room table, tracing the rivers, mountains
and cities so they could find their way in the stories.

She had one small bookshelf that was hers in their bedroom,
where each new collection of a year of reading gathered.
I would sneak them out one at a time.
In seventh grade, I discovered the Holocaust when
I took I Can Never Forgive back to my Saturday of reading all day.
I read every one, haunting my dreams for the next thirty years.

The most vivid moment was one Monday afternoon
as we made dinner and got ready to watch " Laugh In."
This was the one evening we secretly watched television on a school night.
We were safe to break the rules since my father never missed
his Monday night Literary Club downtown,
when the 100 chosen men of Cincinnati gathered
in the elegant house on Taft square
to listen to elaborately constructed papers.

My mother told me about one of the Latin American stories
she'd just read. She said, "It was the strangest thing.
There was this man going on strange adventures and dreaming.
At the end of the story,
the man walks into a wall of flames and when he doesn't burn
he suddenly realizes
that he is a character in someone else's dream."

I felt chills slipping down my spine,
my world of a teenager in the 60s in Ohio split open.
In that moment I was so relieved to discover there was so much more to life
than I'd ever imagined. From then on I began following the tracks of
dreams.

In college, reading Borges' Labyrinths I felt a curious tingling
as I read a story that was already familiar.
Or had I dreamed it? Then I remembered.
This was the story my mother had told me when I was fifteen.

In my 50s in Buenos Aires, I climb the tiny spiral staircase
into the crowded loft of Internet cubicles,
above the roar of traffic on Avenida Corrientes
to discover a friend has emailed Borges' poem
 "The Dream." I feel that same Borges chill
when his poem speaks to me,
tracking me down in his beloved city.

"Who will you be tonight in your dreamfall
into the dark, on the other side of the wall?"

Back at home in my little town in Maine,
I dream inside Borges' Buenos Aires.

I am lying on my back in feather softness,
held by an unseen hand.
floating through a city,
midway between cobblestone streets
and the arching canopy of sycamores,
past wooden shuttered windows opening
into rooms of old carved furniture and mystery.

I awake to the dream of summer in Maine.
The first day to emerge from the amnesia of winter,
when we remember that summer will come:
the washed clear light,
the dry smell of salt crushed shells,
the shimmering sea.

What the Acupuncturist Discovers in Tango

We take our patient's wrists
 to feel the six pulses on each side,
so many times during each treatment,
following the movement of their life
flowing beneath our delicate touch.
These rivers of energy lead us
to what calls out to be moved by the silver needles.
We focus, alone in our own listening,
into the pulses all day long, year after year.

When a student visits, they stand across from us
and we both place our fingertips to the pulses.
We close our eyes, listening to the pulses at the same time,
sinking below the surface into this tangle of currents..
After the treatment, when the blocks are cleared
we look up excitedly, smiling across our patient,
sharing this window into the silent rivers,
feeling them coming more alive.

When I join hand to hand to dance,
pulled firmly into the embrace,
foreheads gently drawing together,
we pause, listening to each other,
waiting before any movement.

Here is someone who has learned to listen like I have,
two practitioners listening to the pulse created
by two dancers joining to dance.
There is no one in the middle.
Two beings meeting,
listening into this distinct pairing
waiting to discover what will be created
in this moment of moving together
inside this poignant call of music.

Learning the Boleo
(with gratitude to Homer and Charity and Providence Tango)

It's as cool as learning to ride my bike
with no hands!
My friends and I circle round and round on our little bikes
in the innocence of a summer day in the early 60s.
We line up and take off, going fast enough
to balance and let go of one hand,
then the other
and we are flying.
Arms out, slicing through the muggy heat of Ohio
making our own cool breezes.
Laughing in the happiness of our great daring.

It's just the same learning the Boleo.
Turning our bodies this way and that,
tracing our foot over the polished floors,
snaking around our standing leg
building up a momentum
building a trust in the language of touch
partner to partner finding our right contact
building trust in our balance,
our hips shimmying from the sway of their shoulders,
we snake our foot round and round,
readying, finding just that right dance
of turning and pressures and momentum,
finding the turning point
and then it happens,
our leg turns back and whips airborne
leaping out of the pull of gravity,
licking through the air halfway up our body,
a flicking bend of knee, a moment's pause
before folding itself in
and tucking its way back to the ground.
We throw our heads back laughing in such delight.
We can't wait to try this again and again,

Riding round the block, our arms flying over
our heads. Look Ma, no hands!

The Boleo:
This elegant Tango step occurs when there is a quick change of direction
and the woman kicks one leg with the knees close together, either to the
back or to the front.

Take This Vow

The first warm day when the lilacs release their scent,
stop going where you thought you were going.

Take that first extravagant blossom of lilac
between both your hands like your lover's face
drawing in the long slow pull of that soft scent.

Turn away from downtown, and head down tree-lined streets, searching.
Fnd the double-headed purple blooms' thick luscious scent.
The shy delicate white lilac reaches over the fence, waiting
for you to draw down to your face the pale thin scent.
Find the old-fashioned lilacs sprawling along the foundations
of the old farmhouses. Spread out your arms,
and sink into the warm fullness wrapping around you.

This is bliss.
Every spring,
a beginner again.

Lilac Night

Stepping out past the magnetic pull of home and light,
remembering warm night walks from childhood,
we think the spring night will be familiar,
that everything will look just like last year.
but following the currents in the lilac night
in the stretches between streetlights
on these back alleys of the 19th century
my neighborhood becomes unknown, frightening.
The borders of evergreens have suddenly grown voluminous.
The trees arch dangerously over the road.
Thickets of shrubs vanish houses without a trace,
Leaves toss white eyed in the glare of the rare mercury street light.

What grows is so urgent to expand, to persist,
to overtake every inch of soil, grasping the advantage of sun.
We are just carving paths out from the wilds.
The moment we stop our gardening it will all fill in,
just give all this growing a little time.
The great overtaking of earth will be covered over,
tangled over, breaking down, fodder for soil,
for more growing, this urge for growing
that persists, reborn each spring
when the scent of lilacs thickens the air.

The Day After She Finishes Driver's Ed My Daughter Suddenly Notices I Write Poetry While Driving

"What are you doing? You can't write and drive!"
She's aghast, watching my pen scrawl across the open notebook
on my lap, as I drive one handed north up Route 1.

"Mimi, I've written nearly half of all my poems while driving
since before you were born. When else can moms write poetry?
I'm completely focused on the road and another part of my mind
is free to write. It's great!"

"I want all your mind on the road!
I don't want to die just because you have to write poetry!"
She pulls the paper and pen out of my grasp.

"Mimi, it's not just for poems. It's for making grocery lists,
and making sure I don't forget things, like that you need ballet shoes.
And lots of people drive and eat!
Please may I have my paper and pen back?"

"No! You can eat and drive, but no poetry!"
She says with determination as we continue up the coast.
I'm left empty handed, soothed by the billowing
indigo wash of lupine in meadow grasses following the road.

An expanse of white paper stretches out in my mind
and no way to etch the day across it.
I have to be patient until I drive off alone
and can once again save my life with poetry.

Listening Inside Island Time

*With gratitude for the generous invitation
of Anina Porter Fuller's Art Week
to spend the last week of June on
Great Spruce Head Island on Penobscot Bay
off the coast of Maine*

Listening Inside Island Time

4:30 A.M.

so light, it's as if there was never any darkness
leave the softness of well worn sheets,
leave the big house with 14 sleeping artists,
step out in my nightgown to go down to the edge of the sea

4:45 A.M.

push open the great old door quietly
emerge from the screenporch into warm blanket of stillness
a world edged in misted islands floating in a silver sea
dawn's half moon high overhead borrowing a tinge of pink
through the meadow grass to the woods,
squat to pee into the crisp of lichen and spruce needle woven path

5:00 A.M.

on the sloping ledge, coolness lifts from the saltwater
swirls of yellow pine pollen snake along the edge of stone and sea
a haze of lush paleness shrouds the horizon
a faint uprising of rose light drifts upwards slowly becoming more

5:15 A.M.

a small darker swirl of rose arises, becomes red becomes an edged circle
of light becomes a solid circle of wild rose redness and the rising
above becomes fuller, expanding and breeze of coolness ruffles
water into rose swathes of velvet laid over silvered satin sea

5:30 A.M.

a sound of a steady downpour raining below the surface of the beach
taking off soft embroidered nightgown to walk into the sea
crisp slippery slip and click of wet smoothed stones
bright delicious chill of saltwater, electric fired wetness on calves
crouching, splashing arms, face, slowly sinking deeper
immersing vulva and buttocks tingling cold etching hint of belly
refreshing aliveness reverberating upward
watching sun rising into golden rose

5:45 A.M.
drying off in the suddenly stilled morning air, watching the cascade of spruce
down to stone-edged shore, trees filled with the calling out
of osprey chicks and the remote heavy rumbling breathing of waves
on an unseen unimagined beach far from this utter still calm expanse of water
where not ever the loon arising into sheen of peach ruffles the surface

6:00 A.M.
up on the crackled ledges, white gold sun rising over a white gold pour
threading out into the cool of silver sea, the peppery staccato of gulls,
the undulating minute bubbling surprise of seaweed snuggling in and out
a single deep mammalian breath out around the cove unseen seal visiting

6:15 A.M.
stepping up the slipping sliding stones to the forest
the softened path bordered with bouquets of ferns and mussel shells
silent stepping through soft meadow grasses curving toward
the weathered gray shingled expanse of opened windows
still silent with rich sleeping awakening quiet

6:30 A.M.
sitting on sea facing screen porch, the sun rising higher
draws out the scent of wild roses just off the porch
bee humming, mosquito stealthy singing, the only conversations

6:45 A.M.
the sun rises above the porch view,
the scent of rose vanishes into a simple smell of warm meadow grass
the bee flies south past the porch and away

7:00 A.M.
the first muffled steps in the kitchen
the faint crumple of newspaper,
the scent of just lit paper and kindling catching

7:15 A.M.
rattle of woodstove grows more confident
sounds of flames crackling
water flushes upstairs
a first step on the balcony

7:30 A.M.
the first voice is heard, "I was so tired from the first day"
the sea still silver, cool streams of air rise through the warmth
bringing the smell of salt

7:45 A.M.
the first lobster boat carves the horizon,
etching the morning with rumbling, pausing, turning round
followed by the arching voices of gulls

8:00 A.M.
the boat slips out of sight,
the silence punctuated by the remote unexpected complaint
of sheep across islands, incredulous, listening intently, waiting,
yes, confirming, those are sheep! bringing the first laughter of morning

8:15 A.M.
screen door slaps open
rustling voices murmuring through the house
Brita asks, "Did you hear that first bird call at 3 a.m.
when it was still pitch dark?"

Stories from the Island at the Edge of the World

Here we ride in our island lifeboat,
cast adrift from the steady moorings of our days
to let the stories drift to the surface.
To let the smell of oils,
the silky powder of pastels against the thumb,
the focusing of the lens and the carving of words
sail us out beyond our known world.

The stories turn mythic
arising among strangers on an island.
Anina tells of following her uncle Eliot as he photographed
birds' nests, and then she carried the nests home to their summerhouse,
lining the walls of her childhood where she still sleeps 60 years later.
She said the songbirds were so thick,
their song so pervasive, and now so rare.
Just the call of gull and crow and an occasional wren.
It is the silent spring, she says with grief.

Telling of inhabitants of the island across the reach,
Brita tells of the pregnant Margaret Fuller and her Italian count
sailing in a storm in the North Atlantic.
When the call went out for women and children to be saved
she chose to throw her journals in the life raft,
and went down with the ship in the arms of her husband.

The next story is of the young and reckless Bucky Fuller
after squandering his inheritance, and killing his young daughter
with his neglect, he walks into the sea at night,
standing up to his neck holding his pistol to his head,
ready to do himself in doubly.
Staring up into the sky of stars he finally stares full face
into the tragic mystery of his life,
and vows to learn everything there is.
To try to make sense of his life, his daughter, to understand
why his Aunt made the choice she did, to slip into the sea.

The story slips in among the china at the vast dinner table
snakes around the hand caned chairs and settles reverberating
through a story I have carried like an old Rookwood vase
that I have turned carefully in my hands for 50 years,
and at this table the story shifts perspective.

There is my great grandmother on the deck of the Lucitania
after the crumpling thud of the torpedo, the listing beginning.
The frantic crying out, Women and children to the lifeboats!

I don't know how long she stood in that brief vast chilling moment of choice.
The story says she was last seen walking arm and arm with my great grandfather,
calmly returning to their stateroom, leaving my grandmother alone
at 19, in college to wake up to their vanishing into the North Atlantic.

We sit at the table of the grandparents, the uncles and aunts,
the paint-spattered easels still on the porch, the photographs on the wall,
the poems to be read next to the fire, and we hear the stories continue.
Anina tells of the paths designed 90 years ago to trace the edges and heights of the island,
the choices made to not cut the woods, to let the trees crash and rot where they fall,
to create soil for the millennia ahead, rather than cutting, which washes the soil away.
It does leave a tinderbox, and if it burns that will be what happens.
We keep the trees back from the houses as best we can,
but it's a risk we take.

The candles are lit. Bowls of ripe peaches and blueberries sweeten
the rising fog disappearing the islands across the reach.
In the story Bucky Fuller heads into a library to read,
beginning with the farthest reaches of the universe,
continuing through everything until he reaches the microscopic.
He emerges with one word. Integrity.
That is what holds it all together.
That is why, he thought, my aunt made her choice.
I think, suddenly understanding, that is why my great grandmother made her choice.

I look around this table of travelers
who sit at this table at the edge of the world,
in the time of the silent spring,
where the vast colony of barn swallows have disappeared
from the island in the last five years.
We don't know what we will face,
the call to lifeboats,
the call to slip into the dark sea,
the windfall of trees slowly rotting into soil,
the tinderbox.
But we each are held together,
points around the compass of this table
with that one word.
Integrity.

It is what takes us out into the glean of the meadow grasses
to face the day.

It's So Good We Didn't Get What We Thought We Always Wanted

I really wanted that Italian architect with the farmhouse in Tuscany
and the long golden afternoons looking over the hills,
but he's still depressed and self centered and not doing anything with his life.
Thank God I didn't get what I thought I wanted!

Thank God I didn't get the Norwegian shipping magnate who was allergic to dogs,
or the captain of the football team, or my sweetheart from grade school,
or was it high school? All those women I didn't marry, or
the men who didn't ask to marry me, and all those relationships that didn't work out.
I mean, what was I thinking!!
And thank God I didn't get Elton John as my boyfriend!

You know, I am so bloody fortunate
I didn't get the trust fund. My friend with the trust fund
who could buy anything she wanted and did, traveled round the world,
got malaria and dengue fever and altitude sickness trekking in Nepal,
and.lost her balance and hasn't been able to dance since.

And thank God, my mom was one of those healthy food types,
even though the homemade, whole wheat bread and homemade mayo
made my bag lunch all greasy, when all I wanted was to have Twinkies
and baloney sandwiches on white bread
and be just like everyone else!

And you know, some of us wanted a Jaguar,
and one of us got an XKE Jag when we were 19,
and took off from Ohio to Maine, and tried out going 125mph.
but that car came with a heavy price tag, and I would have traded
in that brilliant destructive dad for the car if I could have.

And some of us wanted a canopy bed, and a hidden door
leading to a tower full of trunks and secret treasure
as our secret place to get away,
and never to have to grow up.
It's so good we didn't get what we thought we always wanted.
There are too many around us who didn't grow up,
and I wouldn't give anything to be them.

No one could have made up the story our life has taken.
The twists and turns, the ragged edges, the dead ends,
the beginnings again, with all of us ending here
sitting around this table, facing these islands
waiting to see what there is to create next,
just listening, for what is next.
We couldn't have made it up as good as this.

* with gratitude for the Art Week artists who contributed to this list

The Different Sizes of Silence

1. At North Beach

The silence of heat slowly absorbing into this scatter of softly worn stones and crushed mussels.

The silence of the receding tide dropping so stealthily, the exposed ledge gently surprised by sun.

The silence you didn't even notice until the cormorant scoots raucously across the inlet.

The silence of the faraway schooner under full sail on a windless day, barely moving,
sails shimmering white in front of the fog wrapped islands.

The silence in the arched curve of a broken sea urchin, sun bleached delicate lace of pale purple stitches.

2. In the Big House

The companionly silence between the artist painting cross-legged, leaning over her brush and the seated poet writing on the private sleeping porch.

The silence when the artist leaves and her paintings lean against the walls around the poet.

The silence when the poet leaves and the paintings and poems sit quietly in the light tracing across the canvas floor.

The silence of the painter stretched out in the warm meadow grasses between hawkweed and buttercups napping.

The silence between brush strokes of three painters at their easels on the porch facing the woods.

The different shapes and textures of silence stretching out between poems read aloud in the fire-lit Great hall.

The silence in the night meadow in deep fog, the house casting golden light beams the shape of open double windows out into the soft thickened darkness.

The Time It Takes

*In Gratitude for the wise and loving teaching
of Vicki Cohn Pollard*

The Time It Takes For The Work To Become Effortless
(A Letter to a Beginning Practitioner)

All you have to do is to become completely fascinated with who comes to you to be helped. Listen to all the details of their life and their struggles in the body, and see it all with equal attention and fascination. Be especially focused on seeing all the places you or others might find them irritating or wearing and discover how to love those places more than any other. Be proud of them, encourage them, be thrilled by their efforts, applaud their finally beginning to go for walks, to eat better. Read their first story. Adore them the way we were all meant to be adored and delighted in as a child. Begin now. Then the work will become effortless.

All you have to do is to learn to lean into and completely trust in this medicine. You have to let it help you again and again in your most painful places year in and year out. Keep releasing all that is in the way, so you can live in the river of delight you were born to live. All you have to do is live the truth of who you are. All you have to do is let someone love you in this place where you speak the truth of who you are, as you lean into their loving arms. Begin now. Then the work will become effortless.

All you have to do is to create a community of colleagues who speak the language of this medicine, and begin speaking and writing your truth with them. Let them know when you feel like a fraud, when you feel you know nothing, when you have little miracles, when you are struggling and in pain. Let yourself learn to be completely yourself, and let them love you and find you wonderful and stay connected with them through all of your life. Begin now. Then the work will become effortless.

All you have to do is discover a spiritual practice that holds you and teaches you, and that you can learn to lean into. Discover a language of the ancients that helps you be present to suffering, to so much suffering, your own and in the stories you hear all day. Discover a language you can share when people ask you, how can you bear all of this? Discover a practice that helps you hold steady when your dearest patients die, when you lie awake in an agony of fever, when you fear for your children, when you are cast out into your aloneness. Find a practice that helps you quiet the galloping chaotic horses of your mind. Build the muscle of faith. Learn what it is to exercise and strengthen your faith daily. Begin now. Then the work will become effortless.

All you have to do is discover how to keep your creative channels moving. Try what you've never done before, dance, draw, and learn to listen to Beethoven well. If you dream of painting, then call up a friend for lessons the next day. Keep yourself moving, following your creative stream, because this will heal you. Follow your creative stream because you need to know how to support others following their own waterway, because this is what will heal them. Begin now. Then the work will become effortless.

All you have to do is keep taking the pulses on their wrists, listening into the rivers of their life, and one day you will begin hearing the pulses in your ears as your fingertips inquire into their wrists. Then you will see where they are blocked and what you need to do to treat them. This will take five years. Then the work will become effortless.

All you have to do is learn to see who someone really is, under the story and all its distracting details, under the list of all the symptoms. All you have to do is learn to see who they really are, and hold that for them. They will steadily move forward in your knowing. All you have to do is surrender to being of service to helping return each person to their true self. This will take 10 years. Then the work will become effortless.

All you have to do is risk loving whoever walks in your door, and completely love them from that moment they walk in your door. Then you will know all there is to do to treat them without the agony of trying to figure it out. This will take 15 years. Then the work will become effortless.

All you have to do is know that they are the same as you, that there is no separation, that the river of love is saturating both of you, that the treatment is healing both of you, that each treatment is etching its way into healing all of us. This will take 20 years. Then the work will become effortless.

All you have to do is walk out into the street and see everyone you meet with complete delight, and see them all as the same as you, and know that there is no separation. Walk along the street looking up into the buildings, under trees, at every bird and animal you meet, the stones and driftwood along the ocean and love it all and know that this is all aliveness and that there is no separation. This will take the rest of your life. Begin now. Then the work will become effortless.

About the Author:

Elizabeth W. Garber was born in 1953 and grew up in a village in Ohio. She has lived on a square-rigged sailing ship, and on a dairy farm in France. She studied mythology and Greek epic at Johns Hopkins and Harvard, worked as a renovation carpenter in California, and received her Masters in Traditional Five Element Acupuncture and has been practicing this for 20 years in Belfast, Maine.

Her first book of poetry was *Pierced by the Seasons: Living a Life on the Coast of Maine* (2004). Her poem *"Feasting"* from this collection was read on The Writer's Almanac, and is included in Garrison Keillor's anthology, *Good Poems for Hard Times* (2005).

Her previous chapbook collections of poetry are *Finding the Beloved: A Personal Journey to Recover the Divine from Centuries of Devastation* (1991), created along with painted sculptures and performed with a chorus of singers 12 times in New England over two years, including at the University of Maine at Orono and at Harvard Divinity School; *Grabbing Down Deep into the Wailing Room and Re-Emerging Through the Fire* (1993) performed with drummers and a slide show of photographs; *The Salmon Man's Bride* (1993); *At the Moment of Meeting: All Can Be Known* (1994) a series of poems written in collaboration with the artists Robert Shetterly and Louise Bourne for a show of paintings, sculptures, and poetry exploring the themes of the Annunciation at the Frick Gallery in Belfast, Maine.

About the Translator:

Demian Gawianski was born in 1981 in Buenos Aires, Argentina, where he lives today. He is a teacher of Spanish as a Second Language, became fluent in English at a young age, and is dedicated to the study of different languages and cultures, currently studying German and Chinese. His Bachelor's degree is in Classical Literature (Sanskrit, Greek, Latin) at Universidad de Buenos Aires.

His first book is *Buenos Aires Experience, Enjoy the Tango of Learning Spanish*. It is an Argentine Spanish language course book, mainly addressed to English speaking Tango lovers who want to learn the language in combination with Tango poetry and with the culture of the city.
www.tangospanish.com

Acknowledgements

I am grateful for my friends who encourage my writing, especially Kate Barnes, Nancy Burwell and the Belfast Poetry Project, Diane Brott Courant, Squidge Davis, Martha Derbyshire, Jerri Finch, Anina Porter Fuller and the Art Week 2005 participants, Stephen and Helene Huyler, Alexandra Merrill, Kate NaDeau, Vicki Pollard, Deborah Rose, George Van Deventer, Baron Wormser, my Acupuncture colleagues, my wonderful clients, to Beth and Robin whose encouraging style of teaching Pilates has led me into listening inside the body, and my steadily supportive loving family.

I am grateful for my Tango friends and teachers who made our journey to Buenos Aires so rich: Alicia, Marcela, Meredith and Andres, Lachlan, Alcira, Otilia, Belén, the Providence Tango community, for all those partners who are so patient with beginners and for Pam McKeen, for your enthusiastic support and for the incredible good fortune of suggesting to Demian that he might consider translating these poems.

I especially appreciate the Tango painting collaborations with James Strickland, and Brita Holmquist's generous sharing of her painting for the cover of this book. I'll forever treasure one of the richest literary months of my life receiving emailed translations from Demian Gawianski in Argentina each day. I'm grateful for the elegant graphic design work by Catlin Sayers Barnes, the lively photo session with Stephen Huyler, the thorough copy editing by Elizabeth IlgenFritz, and Ray Estabrook's printing expertise to bring this book into form.